A
Danger of
Democracy

. . . The process of election affords a moral certainty that the office of President will never fall to the lot of a man who is not in an eminent degree endowed with the requisite qualifications . . .

—Alexander Hamilton
The Federalist, Number 68

A Danger of Democracy

The Presidential Nominating Process

Terry Sanford

Westview Press / Boulder, Colorado

Published in 1981 in the United States of America by
   Westview Press, Inc.
   5500 Central Avenue
   Boulder, Colorado 80301
   Frederick A. Praeger, Publisher

Library of Congress Cataloging in Publication Data
Sanford, Terry, 1917-
   A danger of democracy.
   Bibliography: p.
   Includes index.
   1. Presidents—United States—Nomination. I. Title.
JK521.S26   324.5'0973   80-29535
ISBN 0-86531-159-5

Printed and bound in the United States of America

To Margaret Rose

Contents

CONTENTS

Preface

Quail hunters appreciate a bird dog that doesn't give up, that chases the last bird after a covey rises, that is joyously unwilling to let even one get away. Old Pal was such a pointer, and on one day he leaped for a last fluttering single, missed, of course, but, sad to say, leaped also over a sixty-foot cliff into the icy Flint River. The moral is that he was going after the right bird but he wasn't looking where he was going.

The political party, with new rules calculated to open the presidential nominating process, to involve more people, to reach the ultimate in democracy, may find itself in the same plight as the conscientious pointer. It is possible to go over the cliff in reaching for too much democracy. Some think the parties have already fallen into the river.

There is, of course, heretical as it sounds, such a thing as too much democracy in nominating our presidential candidates. The danger of democracy is that too much of it might in time, or at some time, suffocate democracy. In reaching too strenuously for the goal, we could damage or destroy democratic government, especially if we mistakenly assume the goal to be participation rather than a democracy's way of selecting the best possible presidential candidates.

As we watched the 1980 campaign for the presidential nominations, the inevitable conclusion once again was that there must be a better way for a democracy to nominate its leader. It is not that the political parties haven't tried. They have tried too hard. The despair is not new. After the 1968 Democratic Convention and the 1964 Republican Convention a great many students of politics concluded that there was something drastically wrong with the nominating process.

We have been rushing for the worthy objective of democracy in full bloom, but it is not equally certain we have been looking where we were going. Reforms in the 1970s generally had the thrust of openness and fuller representation and participation, and they have been justifiably applauded. Yet the system is still a mess, even if for different reasons from those that brought chaos to the Democrats in 1968. It is now time to draw back, to look where we are going, to redirect the system to its intended purpose: presenting the best possible presidential candidates to the voters.

The purpose of this study is to lift lessons from the fascinating history of party nominations in the United States, to suggest some conclusions about present inadequacies, to propose a new concept or philosophy, and to recommend that we adhere to three new principles in the nominating process. The two major political parties can implement these principles by simple changes in their rules.

The way we pick our presidents should not be fraught with danger and uncertainty. It should be a clear, secure, sensible procedure in which we can have confidence and through which an orderly expression of the opinions of an ever-increasing number of interested citizens is assured.

I do not propose doing away with conventions. I do not propose doing away with primaries. I do not propose amending the rules of state allocations, delegate challenges, affirmative action, or the mechanics of the process, for they will be monkeyed with, tuned, and retuned before and after every national convention both parties are yet to hold. This is not a book about party reform.

I propose a different concept in nominating presidents. It is democratic, and it is republican; it is based in tradition and history, and it is radical. There need be very few changes in what we do now. Essentially I would have us keep our primary elections and caucuses; our openness, fairness, representativeness, and affirmative action; and our wild, flamboyant, exciting conventions. The difference will be that the voters will find themselves seeking the best man or woman for the presidency of the United States instead of having the choices thrust upon them by chance and luck, some good and some bad.

Terry Sanford
Duke University

Acknowledgments

I am indebted to a number of people who read the manuscript of this book, or part of it, and made thoughtful and helpful suggestions. James David Barber, Frederick N. Cleaveland, Lawrence C. Goodwyn, Richard H. Leach, William L. Green, Jr., and Cecil Sanford gave me encouragement and wise counsel when they read the first draft. Political practitioners, including Robert S. Strauss, Jean M. Westwood, Julian Scheer, Martha C. McKay, John H. F. Hoving, Judy L. Love, and Ralph M. Byers, all made extremely helpful suggestions, pointing out many practical difficulties, most of which I have tried to overcome. Neil O. Staebler, former member of the Federal Election Commission, provided me with a detailed analysis of my suggestions, much of which I worked into the manuscript, but I absolve him of liability for the final results. Judith H. Parris of the Library of Congress, formerly of the Brookings Institution, gave me the benefit of page-by-page suggestions, which has made this a far better book.

A number of old friends and associates, including Richard

Adler, John Ehle, Edward J. Gerrity, Jr., and John V. Lindsay, were also good enough to read the manuscript, giving me their impressions and thoughts, which helped sharpen the narrative and the presentation. Richard Cummings, Susan Furniss, Dorothy Lyon, and Eugene J. McCarthy made insightful comments on the crucial chapter dealing with recommendations, and I am grateful to them for their interest and assistance. Joel L. Fleishman's help was indispensable, as was Eugene McDonald's. I am forever indebted to them all.

I also acknowledge with deep appreciation the careful work of Marsha C. Vick in editing the book, and the diligence of Cathy M. Ward and Martha V. Watson of my law office, who typed the several drafts.

T.S.

A
Danger of
Democracy

1

Bosses at Work

He was a big man, beaming and ruddy. His darting eyes pierced the corners of the room and at the same time enveloped his listeners in warmth and friendship. His expressive, ample hands punctuated his earnest words. By now he was standing in the back of a loft room over the People's Bank, used for years for the lodge meeting of the Benevolent and Protective Order of Elks. He had transfixed the local Democratic county chairman and was telling him what he needed to know, what he would never forget. The man was a visitor and had spent the night before in the upper berth of a Pullman heading westward from Chicago. He hadn't slept much. No room there for a big man to turn and get comfortable, but so be it, that was the first time he had not been able to get a lower. Never mind anyhow, he did not need to sleep. Too many names and facts and places were tumbling about his brain. He had work to do and people to see, to gather up, to convince, to sell and seal.

He had just spoken to the lodge members. They had invited him to come from New York, and they were pleased and stirred by the patriotic phrases and praise of the Elks and impressed to have a national lodge officer visit—the first time ever that they had been so honored. But the big man's interest in the lodge and in the lodge members, for all his cordiality and enthusiasm, was at best indirect and secondary, merely his excuse for being in that part of the country. His burning interest was in the man he now had netted at the back of the hall, and the men like him along the path of the visitor's western travels. It was plain that this was his business, this was his purpose; and his husky finger, crooked like a sickle, waved as if determined to reap and then to gather in all the sheaves. The small man in the black suit would control the election of a delegate to the National Democratic Convention the next year—might even decide to be that delegate himself. Furthermore, he was especially worth stalking down because he knew all the other county chairmen in the state, and he was, by all reports, highly regarded by his Democratic colleagues.

The traveler had sat the day before in the ornate office of a mayor, perfectly at ease, exuding confidence, assuring the mayor that the Democrats had the greatest vote-getter in the history of the country. It had been the same when he had visited with a former senator in a law office apparently decorated in the nineteenth century and last dusted the week of the World War I Armistice. "Senator, we can win the election. Let me show you the New York election figures." Not that the senator had not seen them. The visitor, months before, had sent out the full record to every Democratic official and party officer, from the precinct up, in the path of his present travels and, for that matter, all across the nation.[1]

Jim Farley was on the move—buttonholing, convincing, remembering names, making friends. He did not worry about television. There was none. He did not worry about presidential primaries; few people, if any, viewed them as a serious path to the White House. He was out to meet the bosses, the party leaders, knowing that they and not their constituents (if they had any) would determine the nominee for the Democratic party. His mission was to sell Franklin Delano Roosevelt to the handful of party leaders who would select or influence the selection of the delegates to the National Democratic Convention. Farley later wrote:

> The long trip across the continent, although arduous and tire-some, was really invaluable because of the personal knowledge it gave me of the individuals who controlled the party machinery. Between leaving and returning to New York, I shook hands with thousands of men and women, and among them were over 1,100 individuals who held "key" positions in the party. That is, they were state chairmen, country chairmen, and local leaders, or occupied some other position that gave them authority.[2]

James A. Farley had some favorable winds blowing for him. Governor Roosevelt had been reelected by a landslide. The Hoover administration was visibly cracking apart. But it was not to be all smooth sailing. It never is. Ambitious men had other plans. Al Smith, whom Roosevelt had twice nominated in convention, wanted the nomination again and another shot at the now-vulnerable Herbert Hoover.[3] Smith and his friends would in time attempt a fierce effort to "stop Roosevelt."

William G. McAdoo of California, twice almost nominated for the presidency, was supporting the Speaker of the House, John Nance Garner of Texas,[4] and McAdoo was in a position to deliver the California delegates with the help of William Randolph Hearst, or perhaps it was the other way around. McAdoo was the boss, wise and experienced, highly regarded, and a national figure, and it mattered not that there was a California presidential primary. It was a mere formality to reinforce the will of the party bosses led and directed by Hearst and McAdoo, who, incidentally, had reason to despise Alfred E. Smith.

There were other primaries, but a reading of the accounts indicates that the 1932 convention, as the Democratic conventions had been since 1832, was a bosses' convention.

There is not even a recorded serious contention that this was not the best and a completely acceptable process. The only rising demand for change was for the elimination of the costly two-thirds rule.

The voice of the voters was, nonetheless, having a decisive influence on the attitudes and inclinations of the bosses. The 1930 elections not only had seen Roosevelt reelected as governor of New York by a handsome sweep but had brought a general upheaval to the benefit of Democrats in numerous states from Connecticut to Oregon to New Mexico. The repeal of the Eighteenth Amendment was a factor in most of the elections of that year, and it was obvious that the pendulum was swinging toward repeal, a position firmly espoused by Roosevelt. The bosses were listening. The Democratic state and local leaders began to smell victory, something they had neither smelled nor tasted since 1916. Governor Roosevelt had been the Democratic vice-presidential nominee in 1920, and he was well known.

In Alaska the first delegates pledged to Roosevelt were instructed by the Democratic Territorial Convention to vote for Roosevelt, obviously directed by a small group of party leaders with whom Farley had diligently corresponded. On the same day in January of 1932 the Democratic State Committee of North Dakota endorsed Roosevelt and selected a slate of delegates for that state's Democratic primary. It is interesting that Farley considered the matter closed and North Dakota pledged as of that date, without any passing concern about the outcome of the later primary vote.

There were seventeen Democratic primary elections that year, but nowhere in his account of his preconvention campaign does Farley mention them more than parenthetically, and the topic "primaries" is not even to be found in the index of his book, *Behind the Ballots*. That primaries "were not of great significance to Franklin Roosevelt" is confirmed by Gerald Pomper, who placed the 1932 Roosevelt campaign in the category of "unaided by primaries."[5]

4

Actually, Roosevelt lost in the California primary to John Nance Garner and in Massachusetts to Alfred E. Smith, but these events had no appreciable influence on the preconvention campaign. That he won primary elections in "New Hampshire, Georgia, and one or two other states"[6] also appears to have had negligible influence, for his strategy was to rely on the party leaders. The bosses of California and Massachusetts did disturb Farley, and his failure to have them in pocket warned him that very probably he could not deliver a two-thirds majority on the first ballot, as he had been claiming. But had there been no primaries in those two states, it is unlikely that Farley would have been able to wrest the delegates from the Al Smith coterie of Massachusetts politicians or to undermine the determined influence of William Randolph Hearst, who, through his newspapers, was promoting Garner in California. It is safe to conclude that the so-called political bosses had far more influence on the primaries than the primaries had on them.

The rules of the Democratic party required a two-thirds vote to nominate. This had been the rule of the party since its beginning, although the Republican party and its predecessors had always favored a simple majority rule. Although the two-thirds rule may have forced a higher degree of deliberation in the beginning, it had begun to grate on the mechanism to a damaging degree.

In 1920 there had been 44 ballots at the convention, with William G. McAdoo always first or second until James M. Cox, who had run third through the first 6 ballots, finally received the necessary two-thirds majority. As if this ordeal had not been enough, for both the party and McAdoo, the 1924 Democratic Convention had 103 ballots, with McAdoo leading for 85. John W. Davis of West Virginia, who had run no better than third for 99 ballots, took the lead on the 101st ballot.[7] This procedure, the Democrats were beginning to understand, was no way to win elections. It was the specter of deadlock that faced James A. Farley in 1932, and he proceeded to deal with the party bosses from the various states with the assumption that a few leaders could change and shift the delegations. And they could, indeed.

Farley did not need to consider what he might sell to the voters of California. He needed only to sell McAdoo and a few other leaders. Unable to do this immediately, he protected his goodwill, knowing he would later need it to get beyond the two-thirds barrier. McAdoo, twice a victim of the rule that permitted bosses and mayors, senators, governors, and chairmen to deal and wheel and maneuver and trade, was the warning of the danger and the promise of success. The fate of the 1932 convention would again be decided by the same leaders, or their successors. Jim Farley's strategy was to be sure that he had enough of the bosses, and firmly at that, so that successive ballots would not erode his pledges and, in addition, that he retained the favor of other camps so they would not resist shifting to Roosevelt.

At the convention in Chicago eight names were placed in nomination.[8] The stop-Roosevelt people were mostly Smith-inspired. There is bitterness when a protégé challenges the master, and later, when the convention was over and done, Smith did not wait to congratulate Roosevelt. Also, stopping Roosevelt was the first step toward getting the nomination for Smith. The mayors of Newark and New Haven and Waterbury, a congressman from New Jersey, and the Tammany Hall bosses were, among others, whipping up support for Smith. Farley had young Paul V. McNutt scuttling the Tom Taggart machine, replacing the old bosses with new bosses, and delivering Indiana for Roosevelt. The lieutenant governor of Texas was busy getting the votes of his state lined up for Roosevelt, just in case Garner withdrew. It was a bosses' convention. Alfred E. Smith had been nominated by the bosses. Woodrow Wilson had been nominated by the bosses. Nominations were the business of the party bosses.

Nearly a century and a half earlier, in 1796, two parties had been emerging. One, headed by Alexander Hamilton and

John Adams, believed in, or rallied in support of, the Constitution. They called themselves Federalists. The Constitution wasn't handed down from a Mount Sinai, and it wasn't written and accepted without difficulty, differences, and political bitterness. The Articles of Confederation were abandoned reluctantly by many, who feared centralization of the revolutionary government and who coveted the independence of the individual states. It was on these differences that two embryonic parties were formed: the one whose members proclaimed themselves Federalists, and the other whose members were dubbed Anti-Federalists by the opposition. Thomas Jefferson was in the latter group, its leader in fact, and in time he preferred the name Republican to suggest something opposed to a central government with power to override the will of state governments.

Nor was the concept of nominating presidential candidates revealed in a flash of lightning from a cloud. It was anticipated by the Constitution that electors would elect the president and the vice-president and that the individual states would "appoint" electors "in such manner as the legislature thereof may direct."[9] How were electors to receive their instructions? They were to exercise independent judgment. If they could not provide a majority for one individual, the Constitution provided that the five highest on the list would be voted on by the House of Representatives. The electors thus would be the nominating body. This was not likely to be a satisfactory solution, for the Constitution also provided that each state, for this purpose, would have only one vote in the House of Representatives, whereas the number of electors each state had was based on the total number of senators and representatives.

Party nominations were not anticipated but became needed, and so they were invented. The electors, selected in various ways devised by the individual state legislatures, somewhat gradually began to hew to the party line, supporting the candidate who had the nomination of the party whose ticket

7

the individual elector had run on or had favored.

There were no political parties and no reason for nominations in 1789 or four years later, for it was assumed that George Washington should be the first president.[10] By the time Washington was completing his second term, political differences had created two political groups distinct enough to be identified. Most members of Congress identified themselves with Hamilton and his friends, the Federalists, who wanted to influence the selection of electors in favor of their political inclination for president. Thomas Jefferson wanted to stop the Federalist trend; in fact, he wanted to be president.[11]

This was the beginning of political party presidential nominations. The candidates were nominated by members of Congress meeting in informal caucus by political party, the Federalists and the Republicans. In 1796 the Federalist caucus nominated John Adams and Thomas Pinckney, meaning for president and vice-president, respectively, but until the Twelfth Amendment the Constitution did not permit this separate designation. Thomas Jefferson, the nominee for the presidency by the Republican caucus, received the second-highest number of electoral votes and consequently was elected vice-president, which was not the result the electors wanted and probably not an efficient way to run a government. Adams received 71 electoral votes; Jefferson received 68, and Pinckney and Aaron Burr received 59 and 30, respectively.[12]

Four years later President Adams was again nominated by the informal caucus of Federalist members of Congress. The Republicans in Congress, now becoming the majority party, nominated Jefferson for president and Burr for vice-president. Each received 73 electoral votes, thus throwing the election into the House of Representatives even though both candidates were from the same party. Ultimately, the House selected Jefferson.

The Constitution was amended in 1804 to require the

8

separate designation of president and vice-president, but for the 1800 election it took thirty-six ballots in the House of Representatives, the intervention of Federalist Alexander Hamilton, and more to prevent lame duck Federalist congressmen from embarrassing Jefferson, and thwarting the intention of the Republicans, by electing Burr president.[13]

The Republicans, most readers will know, went through the name changes of Democratic-Republican and then Democratic, as they are known today. The Federalists were losing congressional strength, as was indicated by the 1800 election, and accordingly were the first to abandon the congressional caucus as the means of nomination.

In 1808 and again in 1812 the Federalists held a "convention," really a broadened caucus. Neither meeting was generally publicized; in fact both were held in intentional secrecy. Delegates were selected, appointed, or self-appointed in a variety of ways, but essentially they constituted a grouping or gathering of the remnants of the Federalist leadership.

The Republicans, in the ascendancy, continued to use the congressional caucus in 1800, 1804, 1808, 1812, and 1816, although party leaders not in Congress raised more and more protests. The party nominees for those years—Jefferson twice, James Madison twice, and James Monroe once—were all elected. In 1820 Monroe was reelected without opposition, the only person in history other than George Washington so elected. There was no nominating caucus that year.

In 1824 there was a change, partially because there was growing dissatisfaction with the exclusiveness of the caucus method and partially because there were Republican aspirants who had no chance of receiving the congressional caucus nod and thus ambitiously sought other methods to get their names before the electors.[14] The Federalist party was dead. The Republican aspirants were numerous.

William H. Crawford, secretary of the treasury under President James Monroe, resident of Georgia but born in

Virginia, had the edge in 1824 in the congressional caucus, and in fact was nominated, but only 68 of the 260 congressmen participated. Even congressmen were beginning to oppose the congressional caucus, and most of those for candidates other than Crawford ignored the caucus. The congressional caucus was discredited and never again used.

Other candidates and their supporters sought other nominating authorities. The legislature of Tennessee nominated Andrew Jackson, and the legislatures of Missouri and Kentucky nominated Henry Clay. The Maine and Massachusetts legislatures nominated John Quincy Adams, and John C. Calhoun was nominated by the South Carolina legislature. The electors then faced a choice among five Republicans (also known as Democrat-Republicans) and no Federalist.

The electors, selected in 1824 by the voters in eighteen states and appointed by the legislature in the six others, voted for four candidates, Calhoun having withdrawn to the vice-presidential slot. No one received a majority. Jackson led with 99 votes to Adams's 84; Clay received 37, and Crawford, 41. Again the House of Representatives had to decide. Crawford had suffered a stroke, and Clay supported Adams, so Jackson was dealt out. Thirteen states voted for Adams; seven for Jackson; and four for Crawford.[15]

The historical significance of the 1824 nominations and election is that that year marked the end of the congressional caucus system and the beginning of a search for a more democratic and a more representative method of nomination. It was a long and shifting path from Jackson's nomination by the Tennessee legislature to Jim Farley's marshaling of the party bosses to nominate Franklin Roosevelt. More people were involved with Roosevelt's nomination than with Jackson's, but a process that was open, representative, and democratic had not yet been achieved.

Roosevelt defeated Herbert Hoover overwhelmingly and

electrified the depressed nation with his inaugural challenge, "The only thing we have to fear is fear itself." The bosses had done a good job.

Notes

1. John T. Casey and James Bowles, *Farley and Tomorrow* (Chicago: Reilly & Lee Co., 1937), p. 135.

2. James A. Farley, *Behind the Ballots* (New York: Harcourt, Brace and Company, 1938), p. 87.

3. For a description of the Roosevelt nomination in 1932, see Farley, *Behind the Ballots*, pp. 58–154.

4. Arthur M. Schlesinger, Jr., *The Crisis of the Old Order: 1919–1933* (Boston: Houghton Mifflin Company, 1957), p. 286.

5. Gerald Pomper, *Nominating the President* (Evanston: Northwestern University Press, 1963), pp. 107–108.

6. Farley, *Behind the Ballots*, p. 100. This was the way Farley summarily dismissed his primaries, although in 1932, of the seventeen Democratic primaries, Roosevelt's name was entered in fourteen. He carried eight with no or insignificant opposition; got about 57 percent of the vote against Smith in Pennsylvania with the help of Joseph Guffy of Pittsburgh; beat Garner in Nebraska about three to one; lost, along with Smith, to Garner in California; lost to a favorite son in Illinois; and lost to Smith one to three in Massachusetts and by 3,219 to 5,234 in New Jersey (see James W. Davis, *Presidential Primaries: Road to the White House* [New York: Thomas Y. Crowell Company, 1967], p. 289).

7. Richard C. Bain and Judith H. Parris, *Convention Decisions and Voting Records*, 2d ed. (Washington, D.C.: Brookings Institution, 1973), pp. 212–213 and 222–224.

8. For fuller description, see Bain and Parris, *Convention Decisions and Voting Records*, pp. 238–244.

9. U.S., *Constitution*, Art. II, sec. 1.

10. The electors for the first presidential election were picked by the legislatures in six states, by the voters in three, and jointly by the legislature and voters in one; the New York legislature was deadlocked and

named none, and North Carolina and Rhode Island did not participate because they had not ratified the Constitution (Eugene H. Roseboom, *A History of Presidential Elections* [London: Macmillan Company, 1957], pp. 15 and 16).

11. Joseph Charles, *The Origins of the American Party System* (New York: Harper & Row, 1956), pp. 91–103.

12. For an account of the 1796 election, see Page Smith, "Election of 1796," in *History of American Presidential Elections*, vol. 1, *1789–1844*, ed. Arthur M. Schlesinger, Jr. (New York: Chelsea House Publishers, 1971), pp. 59–98.

13. Noble E. Cunningham, Jr., "Election of 1800," in *History of American Presidential Elections*, vol. 1, *1789–1844*, pp. 132–133.

14. William Goodman, *The Two-Party System in the United States* (Princeton, N.J.: D. Van Nostrand Company, 1956), p. 171.

15. James F. Hopkins, "Election of 1824," in *History of American Presidential Elections*, vol. 1, *1789–1844*, p. 376.

2

Participatory Disorder

The scene at Convention Hall in Miami, where Democrats were assembled after more than a year of campaigning, caucuses, and primaries, was enough to dismay the old-timers of the Democratic party. It did indeed dismay and confound them as they observed their party in convention selecting their party's standard bearer. The year was 1972. The "ordinary people" had taken over. Many of the nominal and usual leaders of the Democratic party were not in Miami but back home in front of their television sets. Even if they were there as delegates, the customary leaders were outnumbered by the strange and unrecognizable new crowd.

The party stalwarts snorted, "Who are these people?" They were, on closer examination, ordinary American people, having a wonderful time, caught up in the excitement of a national presidential nominating convention—the first time ever for 85 percent of them.[1] A majority of them came bound in advance, most legally committed, for George McGovern, "although he was the first choice of only 30 percent of the Nation's Democrats."[2]

In attendance were women, blacks, people with Spanish surnames, native Americans, young people (by definition no older than twenty-nine), college faculty members, and activists who had proved their activism by demonstrating against the Vietnam War. Never had there been a group so diverse at a Democratic National Convention. It would have been difficult to find fault with the individual delegates, who had not less and perhaps more intelligence, education, income, and concern than previous delegates. There was, however, something out of sync.

How did it happen? Why did the mayors and governors, senators and party officials feel "excluded"? Why? It was planned that way; surely not totally intentionally but nonetheless planned. The answer did not lie on the Miami convention floor of 1972 but, rather, in events that had their origins four years earlier in the bizarre, colorful, and ultimately tragic Democratic Convention of 1968. In that year, the Democrats had met in Chicago. The delegates had been selected in very much the same way as the delegates who had met in 1964 when Lyndon Baines Johnson was nominated and before that in 1960 when John F. Kennedy was nominated. But 1968 was different.

Campuses were being disrupted. Awareness of the error of the Vietnam War was building across the nation. In 1968 the protesters were mostly young people, and they followed the tactics of the civil rights movement, which was still in full swing. Organized women's groups were finding new and more militant support and insisting that women be freed from all vestiges of discrimination. It was an especially bad time for the Democrats. Demonstrators and protesters had no call to ponder that the Republicans would please them less. The target was now, and the Democrat in the White House was blamed for the Vietnam War.

Senator Eugene McCarthy of Minnesota, relatively unknown, had announced for the presidential nomination against the incumbent president, an unprecedented mode of challenge in this century, except for Teddy Roosevelt's foray against William Howard Taft in 1912. McCarthy had scored a media upset in the New Hampshire primary by gaining 42 percent of the popular vote and twenty of the twenty-four delegates.[3] Robert Kennedy, then senator from New York, reversed his earlier declination and jumped late into the race, entering the primaries where the filing dates had not passed.

On March 31, 1968, President Johnson, for reasons he explained, surprised the nation by announcing he would not be a candidate for reelection. Within a week the vice-president, Hubert H. Humphrey, created a campaign committee, and on April 27 he formally announced his candidacy. It was too late for him to enter many primaries, and anyhow it was not in his interest to do so.

Humphrey had some strengths and some weaknesses. He had the admiration and generally the support of party and public officials and a record of having been his own man in championing the valiant causes that had marked the progress of the nation in the two post–World War II decades. He, unfortunately, did not have the image of being his own man on the issue of the Vietnam War but was suspected of giving in on his principles because his benefactor, LBJ, had made him the vice-president. Humphrey was loyal, prided himself on his loyalty, and did his best to gain understanding and support for President Johnson. To this departure, his former cheering, liberal friends could not adjust.

Demonstrations had become a way of life, and if disruptions resulted, so be it. The disenchanted youth and their older allies saw no other way to stop the war. McCarthy had been the first challenger, so the young people flocked to him. Then the magic of Robert Kennedy captured the rest. Between the two of them they had the attention, they had the issue. Hubert Humphrey was plodding along diligently, with staff and political leaders lining up votes in all the states where that was possible. The system did not put him at a disadvantage. The leaders were the leaders.

McCarthy beat Kennedy in Oregon, and then Kennedy recovered by beating McCarthy in the California winner-take-all primary. Then, suddenly, there was the tragic assassination of Robert Kennedy! The young were bitter, shocked, and outraged. The system, the establishment, somehow seemed responsible for all the strife, and there seemed to be nothing the young could do to turn things around. They were left out of the system, or so it seemed when one was that age, and by the time they were older and part of the system, they too, they feared, would be corrupted by the system. Those were uneasy years, and there were all too few elders who understood the distress and mounting anger of young people.

The mayor of Chicago was not one who understood. His city was to be the host city of his party's national convention. The threats of disruption and the clear and inevitable gathering of protesting young people were challenges, the mayor proclaimed, that would be put down, not allowed. In a series of mistakes he denied young people use of the stadium and the parks, and he mobilized his police force for battle against these unholy and un-American invaders.

Whether there was police brutality, or even whether there was some kind of conspiracy by a small band with ulterior motives to use the wrath of the young people, is now a moot point, and whether wiser official action would have constructively channeled the energy of the young dissidents into a forceful, useful statement against the war is no longer pertinent. The television public saw brutality, disorganized lack of leadership, and a party in disarray. Once brutality, brusqueness, and arrogance are unleashed, the countryside is polluted, and many delegates who were meek and mild, law-abiding, and God-fearing felt the iron hand of repression and hatred. Security for the delegates often seemed to be security against the delegates, as they, too, were shoved and herded and, if stubborn enough to resist, sometimes hustled and dragged. That is what the public saw, understood, and despised. The slinging of billy clubs by the mayor's police in the parks and along Michigan Avenue further presented an ugly eruption that was to be devastating.

The hapless victim was Hubert H. Humphrey, although it might be argued that he could have done more to relax the inflexible arrogance of Chicago's City Hall. He did not and perhaps could not. Neither could he heal, quickly enough, the party wounds that crippled his campaign. As it was to be four years later, luck saved Richard Nixon, and the hapless victim, it turned out, was not Humphrey or the Democratic party but the American people.

A recital of the troubles of the Chicago convention is not relevant to this discussion except that Humphrey, battered and bothered, responded to his defeat and to his concern that the young were probably correct by assuming that he should appoint a committee to put things right. The real complaint of the young was not so much that they were not delegates, but that the war continued, that they lacked the power to do anything about it, and that they were abused when they tried. They were hurt and angry, but it was anger rooted not so much in hatred as in disappointment and despair. The country was going to hell and no one in power, no member of the establishment, was doing anything about it or even seemed to understand what was happening to American society and its moral leadership in the world. They did not seem to care; worse, they resented just listening—and would not—and scolded anyone who would try to tell them what was happening.

Eugene McCarthy would listen, but he already knew, and "they" would not listen to him. He was gentle and kind, almost meek, and the political powers, the "bosses," said that was all a sign of weakness, of softness toward our mortal enemies. They said he did not have the strong characteristics demanded by the presidency—that the meek shall inherit the earth is just something written in the Bible.

The tragedy of Chicago was the brutal disregard of the idealistic yearnings of young people. It was not necessary that the young people come inside the convention hall, but it was necessary to treat them like our own children, which they were, and that we listen and learn and understand that they were not crazies, that they had a message of tremendous import, as history has borne out. The "Democratic establishment's" mistake in the summer of 1968 was to so split the party that there was not time to mend the split before the November elections.

Hubert Humphrey, in defeat, appropriately took charge of the party machinery, selected Senator Fred Harris as the new chairman of the Democratic National Committee, and through him appointed a commission to study the party machinery to make it more representative. A rules change should have been made and was past due, but it was at this point that most party leaders concerned made an error in evaluation.

Had the new rules been in effect in 1968, would there nonetheless have been demonstrators against the war? Would the city of Chicago have exhibited genteel hospitality? Would the police have received different instructions?

It could be argued convincingly that the young were not getting their heads bloodied and their eyes and nostrils gassed because they wanted to be members of the convention.[4] They would have protested the war and condemned the leaders regardless of party rules and convention structure. Their broad complaints were aimed at "establishments" generally, including political parties and especially the Democratic party that controlled the White House. To say that Mr. Humphrey and those in charge of the remnants of the Democratic party overreacted in drawing up the new rules will certainly be disputed, but the Miami convention left a number of party observers, participants, and leaders expressing the opinion that the reforms had gone too far.

I would contend that there is nothing evil about, and not much wrong with, the Democratic party's intentions in revising its rules. If there was overreaction, it was in the proper direction—the development of a party embracing far wider participation. I would argue that even if the 1969 Democratic leadership were pressed to action by a misconception of the meaning of Chicago, they were motivated by the party's general desire to be concerned for all people, all segments of American society. This spirit of universality was a part of Hubert Humphrey's enduring presidential personality and Minnesota heritage. That Hubert Humphrey's ambitions were thwarted in 1972 in Miami by what his good intentions had wrought, I state as a certainty. His Commission on Party Structure and Delegate Selection had changed the rules so that a Hubert Humphrey found it impossible to be a contender for the nomination.

Headed first by Senator McGovern and later by Congressman Donald M. Fraser of Minnesota, the Commission was largely selected by the party chairman, Fred Harris, a self-proclaimed populist, a decent and humane man who was then the U.S. senator from Oklahoma. The commission members set out to eliminate what they perceived to be the causes of the disaster in Chicago. What were the changes they made?

Even if not so recorded in their minutes, they thought the problem was that young people, blacks, women, and Chicanos were battering the doors because they wanted to get in and everything would be all right if they were let in. This was a misconception. The demonstrators and others there were not volunteering for service in the Democratic party, although they were pleased by the prospect. They wanted to exert their influence to stop the war.

True, in the process, they reminded the leaders that the party structure and the delegate selection process were jerry-built and that people left out tend to become alienated. The happy thought emerged that the more people participating, the stronger the party.

It was in this climate that the new rules for delegate selection were written.

19

They provided, among other things, that: only Democratic voters can participate in choosing national convention delegates; no proxy voting is permitted; the unit rule is outlawed; all candidates for delegate must make known their presidential preferences, if any, prior to the selection process; each presidential candidate must approve the delegate candidates running as his or her supporters; delegates must be chosen in a manner which "fairly reflects the division of preferences expressed by those who participate"; no ex-officio or "automatic" delegate slots may be reserved for party notables; . . . [and every delegation must reflect] full participation by all Democrats, with particular concern for minority groups, native Americans, women, and youth.[5]

The plan became known as the McGovern rules, and the chief irritant was the "quota requirement." (Those who have followed subsequent developments are well aware that Senator McGovern denies that he favored quotas.[6]) The insistence on "full participation" was to be the flaw in the new rules. The next question is why would forming a slate balanced in proportion to the elements of the community from which it is drawn be considered a flaw? Is that not the most representative kind of slate?

Those questions raise the central dilemma: Is a balanced slate necessarily representative? True, it appears to be, but actually, deliberate balancing gives us merely a demographic reflection. Does deliberate balancing make a slate of delegates representative of the constituency?

Herbert McClosky's classic study comparing the policy preferences of convention delegates and rank-and-file party identifiers in 1956 found that Democratic delegates were substantially more liberal than ordinary Democratic identifiers, and Republican delegates were comparably more conservative than the Republican rank-and-file.[7]

Jeane Kirkpatrick's study of delegates to the two 1972 conventions . . . found that the differences between the Democratic delegates and the Democratic identifiers were so great that the policy preferences of ordinary Democratic identifiers were much better represented by *Republican* delegates than by Democratic delegates![8]

Austin Ranney, using figures mostly from Kirkpatrick's *New Presidential Elite,* showed that 8 percent of Republican delegates favored "busing to integrate," compared to 5 percent of the Republican identifiers. On the Democratic side, 15 percent of the Democratic identifiers favored busing to integrate, compared to 66 percent of the delegates to the 1972 convention.

On the issue of "stop crimes regardless of accuseds' rights," the Republicans were even Stephen, with 56 percent of identifiers and 56 percent of delegates being in favor of the proposition. On the Democratic side, although 50 percent of the Democratic identifiers would agree with the majority of the Republicans, only 13 percent of the delegates to the 1972 Democratic National Convention would adopt the statement.

In "attitude toward political demonstrators," 8 percent of the Republican identifiers and 14 percent of the Republican delegates in 1972 took a favorable attitude. On the Democratic side, 14 percent of the identifiers were favorable toward demonstrators, but 59 percent, four times as many, of the 1972 Democratic Convention delegates were favorable.[9] Doubtless many had *been* demonstrators.

In part, the dilemma posed by these comparisons arises from sloppy language. "Representation" involves more than a balanced pattern of people, more than a miniature of the community. Representation in the political sense involves accountability and responsibility to a constituency, and at least a general agreement with that constituency's political attitudes.

The sad fact is that McGovern's campaign against Nixon was doomed before the opening gavel had fallen. That McGovern was not representative, that he had no consensus, that he was defeated before he started were not and are not commentaries on his integrity or his political philosophy. He had run by the rules, told the truth about himself, and accumulated a majority of the delegates who were in Miami because of him and on his behalf. His failure, which is to say his success in acquiring the nomination, is not a reflection on him but an indictment of the procedure.

Austin Ranney concluded that "in 1972 the candidacy of George McGovern was opposed by most party organization leaders and supporters because McGovern was thought to be too radical and unelectable."[10] That is, he was *not* representative of his party, let alone the nation, although the rules had dictated that the party must reflect "full participation by all Democrats."

Party leaders, both Democratic and Republican, look for a winner, which is to say they attempt to find among their possibilities a nominee who will be well received, obtain the confidence of the voters, and win. "But the new rules put a premium on the kind of dedicated, issue-oriented army of enthusiasts that McGovern, like McCarthy four years earlier, mobilized."[11]

Certainly George McGovern's campaign, which he started early against considerable odds, will stand as a memorable American success story. He persevered, he raised money, he made believers of the doubters, and he influenced greatly the forces that ended the Vietnam War. Theodore White called the campaign

a national mobilization of irregulars—a masterpiece of partisan warfare, its troops living off the land, tapping veins of frustration everywhere; raising money locally as they rolled; their captains and lieutenants, young men without commissions or epaulets, commanding and creating a net of cells in storefronts, cellars, campuses, kitchens; youth and women organized; all of them recruiting, preaching, persuading, stirring to action hearts hitherto unstirred by politics.[12]

The nominating system should allow such stirring to action, but a campaign and political party are lost without consensus.

No other candidate, with the exception of George Wallace, had such a sharply defined appeal. Neither he nor McGovern could build consensus, but the nominating process favored the direct strategy.

> Clearly, the median position has little appeal, and is in fact quite vulnerable, to a third or fourth candidate contemplating a run against two centrists. This is one lesson that centrist candidates Hubert Humphrey and Edmund Muskie learned to their dismay in the early Democratic primaries in 1972 when George McGovern and George Wallace mounted challenges from the left and right, respectively. Only after Muskie was eliminated and Wallace was disabled by an assassin and forced to withdraw did Humphrey begin to make gains on McGovern in the later primaries, but not by enough to win.[13]

McGovern's campaign success is best illustrated by workers like Joe Grandmaison and Gene Pokorny. Grandmaison was given the crucial responsibility for New Hampshire, and Pokorny's key assignment was Wisconsin. Grandmaison was known in his small native state, but he was young and untried, and his victory for McGovern was viewed as a stunning upset. It mattered not at all that Pokorny was unknown, not a political leader from Wisconsin or anywhere else for that matter. His job was to find and energize the militants who wanted to stop the war. Theodore White pictured Pokorny as

> living in the home of a McGovern loyalist in Milwaukee, dining as a boarder with the family and three children. . . . "Our first task," said Pokorny, "was to consolidate the left." Which meant, specifically, to energize what was left of the McCarthy insurgency that had swept Wisconsin in 1968. It meant meetings in Wausau and La Crosse and Kenosha and Madison and all across the state, of six or eight or ten people at someone's home, and committing

them—"our people were committed in blood." . . . Basically, he
sought teachers, "peace freaks," and then, above all, in Pokorny's
earnest words, intending no pun, "peace-minded, broad-based
housewives."[14]

McGovern won the nomination by means of a group of
delegates that, for all their good intentions and high ideals
and selection in conformity with the rules, was not representative. Consequently he did not have a chance of winning
the general election unless the political winds had so blown
that President Nixon might have defeated himself. The winds
rose, but too slowly. The seriousness of the situation is not
that the Democrats lost, but that the loss demonstrated with
a vengeance the flaw of the philosophy embodied in the new
rules, an abandonment of the need of consensus in order to
gain the nomination.

Eight years earlier the Republicans had contended with the
same kind of doomed nominee, one who had built his partisan
support in advance of the convention, ignoring and even
scorning a consensus. To get the flavor of the Barry Goldwater campaign, we might examine the work of one of his
young California "commanders of the troops," Robert Gaston. "In Gaston's mind, Goldwater was only a beginning and
moderate phase of the conservative revolution that would
come later—and Gaston controlled troops. Since early spring
his troops and operatives had been in action at every level."[15]
Polls showed Goldwater and Nelson Rockefeller swapping
the lead almost daily.[16] Winning was essential to both campaigns. Neither could lose and survive.

> Gaston's legions were organizing for election day. In Los Angeles
> County alone, 9,500 volunteers [were] ready to go from door
> to door on election day to make sure that every indicated Gold-
> water voter marched to the polls to vote for the moral society;
> 10,000 more in southern California; in northern California, 5,000.
> . . . And in the late afternoon of Monday, before the voting,
> churches opened (six in Los Angeles alone) for prayer meetings

for the Goldwater volunteers, that the Lord might bless then in their effort of the morrow.[17]

Goldwater won 51.6 percent of the vote—1,120,403 to 1,052,053 for Rockefeller. Goldwater got all the delegates.

"And with that," Theodore White astutely observed, "the Republican voters had been consulted on their choice for the last time."[18] The Goldwater forces had organized from one edge of the Republican party and had effectively garnered a working majority by the time Goldwater took all the California delegate votes. It was not likely that he could be stopped, and that fact seemed to amaze the established leadership of the Republican party. Until California, Goldwater had not won a contested primary election. He had understood the caucus system, and his determined organizers had done the job. Attracted to Barry Goldwater by his personality, forthright principles, and clear, if narrow, policy positions, those relatively small groups of dedicated campaign workers across the nation—plus about 68,000 voters in California— had handed the United States its alternative without debate.

The Republican leaders, men of considerable position, power, ability, and influence, were thoroughly unhappy with what they saw. There was George Romney, governor of Michigan and eminent businessman, who had dropped out of the presidential race early. There was Nelson Rockefeller, who was on his way out. There was William Scranton of Pennsylvania, one of the brightest young governors in the country. Also there was Richard Nixon, an improbable candidate because of his defeat by John F. Kennedy followed by his defeat in the race for governor of California, but a power. Could those four men agree on one of themselves, or someone else, for a last-minute surge to avoid the defeat and party disarray they were certain Goldwater's candidacy would bring? Nixon went to Cleveland where the Governors Conference was being held, and those four and others closeted themselves and sought a solution. There was none at that late

25

date, or perhaps lingering ambitions prevented agreement. Exasperated, Scranton jumped into the race at the last hour. But the militant, determined delegates, more interested in Goldwater than in the Republican party and not representative of party or nation, were already in place.

It could hardly be contended that Goldwater and McGovern wanted to lose and were more interested in making a point than in being president. Certainly the parties had no such leanings toward martyrdom. This is a question the parties must resolve. Can they have rules that permit martyrdom, intended or happenstance? Can they have rules that permit nomination without enough consensus to assure a reasonable chance of success? A chief purpose of political parties is to establish coalitions and consensus, a vital element of popular self-government. McGovern certainly knew this, but the system had positioned him badly.

Anthony King has suggested that "the American politics have become to a high degree, atomized."[19] This change in our system and our approach makes it far more difficult to identify leadership, far more difficult for candidates to talk sense to the American public.

The continuity of the political party tends to identify leadership, but those people who have the drive to be president have begun to realize that the party leaders are not the source of achievement. The candidates and would-be candidates understand that they must build their own organizations, personally convince the news and editorial media, grab headlines as best they can, draw in special-interest groups where possible, and generally go it alone. Jimmy Carter proved this in 1976. King pointed out that

> leadership becomes more difficult partly because an atomized politics is much harder to understand than a politics of coalition, and is also far more unpredictable. To issue complexity is superadded political complexity. The outcomes of campaigns for presidential nominations always depended on a large number of

factors (including the views of dozens of bosses and state governors, and hundreds of convention delegates); today they depend
on so many factors (including the votes of millions of primary
electors) as to be almost wholly unpredictable. It is no disrespect
to the President to say that, if Jimmy Carter, an ex-Georgia
governor with no national political experience whatever, can win
the presidency, then almost anyone can.[20]

The parties' historic function has been to make political
candidates responsive and understandable. With our present
atomized politics, "it becomes harder for the individual
voter to predict what, in terms of public policy, will be the
outcome of his or her electoral decision. There comes to be
even less connection than there once was between what
voters, even the majority of voters, want and what they
get."[21] Thus, it might be argued that the two major parties,
in attempting to illuminate democracy by their new rules,
have succeeded only in blinding the voters.

Notes

1. Richard C. Bain and Judith H. Parris, *Convention Decisions and
Voting Records* (Washington, D.C.: Brookings Institution, 1973),
p. 332.
2. Ibid., p. 331.
3. Eugene H. Roseboom, *A History of Presidential Elections* (London: Macmillan Company, 1957), p. 588.
4. Indeed, 18 percent of the 1968 Democratic delegates were thirty
years of age and under (Judith H. Parris, *The Convention Problem:
Issues in Reform of Presidential Nominating Procedures* [Washington,
D.C.: Brookings Institution, 1972], p. 59).
5. Austin Ranney, "The Political Parties: Reform and Decline," in
The New American Political System, ed. Anthony King (Washington,
D.C.: American Enterprise Institute for Public Policy Research, 1979),
p. 226.
6. George McGovern, *Grassroots* (New York: Random House,
1977), pp. 144–148.

7. Ranney, "The Political Parties: Reform and Decline," p. 234.

8. Ibid.

9. Ibid., p. 235.

10. Ibid., p. 240.

11. Ibid.

12. Theodore H. White, *The Making of the President 1972* (New York: Atheneum Publishers, 1973), p. 96.

13. Steven J. Brams, *The Presidential Election Game* (New Haven: Yale University Press, 1978), p. 15.

14. White, *The Making of the President 1972*, p. 99.

15. Theodore H. White, *The Making of the President 1964* (New York: Atheneum Publishers, 1965), p. 119.

16. Bain and Parris, *Convention Decisions and Voting Records*, p. 311.

17. White, *The Making of the President 1964*, p. 126.

18. Ibid., pp. 128–129.

19. Anthony King, "The American Polity in the Late 1970s: Building Coalitions in the Sand," in *The New American Political System*, p. 391.

20. Ibid.

21. Ibid.

3

Hail the Conventions

National nominating conventions, the identifiable Mount Everest of the presidential nominating process, did not come by way of George Washington, the Constitution, or a special commission studying ways to open the parties to fuller participation. "No method of nomination was written into the Constitution, since the Founders assumed the choice would be limited to a very small number of obviously well-qualified men and that the best man would win. This system worked, but not for long."[1]

The nominating process had to be invented. It was not seen as a government function, and to this day congressional sanction has never been asserted. The unofficial congressional caucus by party members was originally the only way to gain any unity. Later, and briefly, nominations by state legislatures, more than a solution, indicated a searching for a representative way for party members to express themselves. Conventions, whose time arrived in 1832, seemed to be the answer. Some scholars trace the origin of the delegate state convention to Pennsylvania. In any event the prototype was available in several states when it was called into national service.[2]

The honors for the first national convention went to an unlikely contestant, the Anti-Masonic party, when its members convened in Baltimore on September 26, 1831. Although somewhat obvious, the move was an innovative idea to get attention for the group, which had such a peculiar motivation for establishing a political party. Why a group of otherwise more or less rational men would set out after the Masons is an irrelevancy of history,[3] but the group's members felt that a convention, a utilization of an open process, would bring added public attention, and, besides, the party did not have a candidate. Its leaders needed a convention in order to discuss possible candidates so they might make a reasonable choice.[4] This purpose, I might observe—to discuss the candidates and make a reasonable choice—as useful and praiseworthy as it might seem, has today been effectively abandoned by the Democratic party and is on shaky ground under the rules of the Republican Convention.

The Anti-Masons, having made their contribution to the American political process, passed from the scene after nominating a rather distinguished citizen, William Wirt. In accepting the nomination he declared that he had once been a Mason, a fact of which the convention was already aware, and that he saw nothing insidious in Masonry, George Washington having been a member. Nevertheless he was willing to run for the presidency against Andrew Jackson and Henry Clay—a task that in due time proved to be utterly futile.

In December of that same year, and of more lasting significance, the National Republican party, forerunner of the present Republican party (the former party did not live to hold a second convention), convened a national convention in Baltimore, using for its convention hall the same saloon that had been used by the Anti-Masons.[5] Eighteen states were represented. This too was a new party, with a need for attention that its members hoped a convention would bring.

Banded together in opposition to President Andrew Jackson, their roots partially in the Federalist tradition of Alexander Hamilton, they were spurred on by Jackson's veto of legislation to recharter Nicholas Biddle's national bank. The national bank had been championed in Congress by Henry Clay, and the National Republican Party nominated Clay for the presidency.

That National Republican Convention is credited with having the first nominating speech. It took the form of an "address to the people," which denounced Jackson, praised Clay, and dealt also with some issues. In May of the following year a National Republican Convention of young men, prompted by the December convention, met in Washington, named Clay, heard an acceptance speech by him, and drew up a party platform.[6] Two weeks later in May 1832, the Democratic party held its first convention, solely because President Andrew Jackson wanted to scuttle his vice-president, John C. Calhoun.

In 1828 some Democratic party leaders had discussed the possibility of a convention, but they did not follow through on the idea. "Jackson and Calhoun were placed on the ballot in a rather haphazard way through a series of nominations in state conventions."[7] Jackson did not need a convention to be renominated. He assumed that obviously the electors knew he was a candidate, and he had already been nominated by several state legislatures. Thus the convention felt it was unnecessary to nominate him, and it simply concurred with what the states had done.[8]

The first Democratic Convention (this was the period of transition from the name "Republican" to "Democrat") was called by a resolution of "the Republican members of the New Hampshire Legislature" to be "friendly to the election of General Jackson, to consist of delegates equal to the number of electors of President in each State, to be holden in Baltimore . . . to nominate a candidate for Vice-President." The resolution was instigated by members of the Jackson administration.[9]

> Jackson's choice for the nomination was Van Buren, but the latter was far from being a favorite with the party, and for the purpose of overcoming opposition to him Jackson had decided to resort to the convention system. . . . He then saw to it that most of the delegates chosen should be amenable to advice from himself as to the proper course to pursue, and such as were not in that frame of mind were informed after the convention assembled that it would be well for them to favor Van Buren, "unless they wished to quarrel with the general." As few were anxious to quarrel with that redoubtable personage, he had a very large majority of the convention ready to do his bidding.[10]

Martin Van Buren was selected as the vice-presidential candidate by this convention. The unit rule was adopted. There were no nominating speeches, no platform, no demonstrations. These refinements were to evolve later.

The selection of delegates to these first conventions was somewhat informal. Those attending Jackson's Democratic Convention came from all the twenty-four states except Missouri. There were 326 in attendance, more than the 1 delegate per electoral vote (282) set by the New Hampshire resolution.[11] In subsequent years the delegates were chosen in a variety of ways to represent their party's constituency. There were gradual forward changes, sometimes with setbacks, to make the selections more open to more participants, to make the process more public, to gain attention from the electorate, and to present a candidate the delegates hoped would be a winner.

The conventions for the 1832 election were generally considered to have brought many advantages. A convention, it seemed, "was representative in character; it divorced nominations from Congressional control and added to the independence of the executive; it permitted an authoritative formulation of a party program; and it concentrated the party's strength behind a single ticket, the product of a compromise of personal rivalries and group of sectional interests."[12]

It was not representative by today's standards. Women

were not a part of the electorate, and delegates to the first several national party conventions were selected and seated rather casually. Sometimes delegates were elected by state legislatures, but more often they were selected by state conventions, unorganized caucuses, or just meetings of some party leaders. At the second Democratic Convention, which nominated for president Martin Van Buren, Jackson's vice-president and protégé, Tennessee was not represented, so a Tennessee man who just happened to be in town was recognized and cast the entire vote of that state.[13] It also helped that he was a Van Buren supporter.

Conventions are obviously a handy way to gather in the party leaders to chart a party's course and to place a nominee's name before the public. It was not and still is not necessary for a political party, or a group that calls itself a political party, to have a convention in order to nominate a candidate. Any slate of electors can be placed on the ballot if the statutory requirements of an individual state are met. The Constitution still requires the electors for each state to be appointed "in such manner as the legislature thereof may direct." Much has changed since Henry Clay, William Wirt, and Andrew Jackson were the candidates in 1832, but conventions have remained the culmination of the nominating process.

William Goodman noted in 1956, "The outstanding fact about the national nominating convention is its extralegal character. . . . On its comparative record, the national convention has done well. Its unbroken use since 1840 has established it by the pragmatic test of time. It has worked without statutory regulation or violence beyond epithets and occasional fisticuffs. As an invention it has filled the void created by necessity."[14] But now there are doubts. In 1968 a special Democratic commission observed, "The emergence of the issue-oriented independent has called into question as never before the value of the convention system for selecting presidential nominees, as it has traditionally operated."[15]

33

Reforms have been constantly recommended, and some have been adopted. In 1898 Edward Stanwood wrote about some of the abuses and shortcomings of conventions, recommended some reforms, and admonished his readers as follows. "Consequently it should be the concern of all good citizens to make the national convention, through which parties act directly upon the government, a free and independent body, expressive of the best thought, the highest motives, and the truest patriotism of the party."[16] The parties have wanted to live up to this lofty hope, and they have attempted to reform and improve, but the system has never been in such disrepair.

After 1972 it could be said,

> Conventions are no longer best conceptualized as gatherings of important party members to select a candidate. With the passing of control over delegate selection processes from party to national candidate organizations, conventions have become meetings of individuals with a primary, though varying, commitment to a particular candidacy. The evolution toward candidate-centered conventions suggests the need for a re-examination of much of the established thinking about conventions.[17]

After about a century and a half of conventions the issue is joined. Have conventions outlived their usefulness to the American republic and should they now be abandoned? Or, have we, intentionally or inadvertently, damaged a consensus-building instrument that is crucial to our effective self-government?

Notes

1. Stanford M. Mirkin, ed., *1964 Guide to Conventions and Elections* (New York: Dell Publishing Co. by Columbia Broadcasting System, 1964), p. 11.

2. Edward Stanwood, *A History of the Presidency from 1788 to 1897* (Boston and New York: Houghton Mifflin Company, 1898), p. 170.

3. See Charles McCarthy, "The Antimasonic Party: A Study of Political Anti-Masonry in the United States, 1827–1840," vol. 1, *Annual Report of the American Historical Association for the Year 1902* (Washington, D.C.: Government Printing Office, 1903), pp. 367–574.

4. Richard C. Bain and Judith H. Parris, *Convention Decisions and Voting Records* (Washington, D.C.: Brookings Institution, 1973), p. 14.

5. Robert V. Remini, "Election of 1832," in *History of American Presidential Elections*, vol. 1, *1789–1844*, ed. Arthur M. Schlesinger, Jr. (New York: Chelsea House Publishers, 1971), p. 505.

6. Ibid., pp. 505–507.

7. Ibid., p. 501.

8. Ibid., p. 508.

9. Stanwood, *A History of the Presidency from 1788 to 1897*, pp. 159–160.

10. Joseph Bucklin Bishop, *Presidential Nominations and Elections* (New York: Charles Scribner's Sons, 1916), p. 9.

11. Ibid., p. 160.

12. Eugene H. Roseboom, *A History of Presidential Elections* (London: Macmillan Company, 1957), p. 106.

13. Ibid.

14. William Goodman, *The Two-Party System in the United States* (Princeton, N.J.: D. Van Nostrand Company, 1956), p. 562.

15. U.S., Congress, House, *Report of Commission on the Democratic Selection of Presidential Nominees*, 90th Cong., 2d sess., 14 October 1968, *Congressional Record*, 114:31547.

16. Stanwood, *A History of the Presidency from 1788 to 1897*, p. 177.

17. F. Christopher Arterton, "Strategies and Tactics of Candidate Organizations," *Political Science Quarterly* 92 (Winter 1977–78):670.

4

Bosses and Dark Horses

The upheavals of the Civil War contributed to realignment of the political parties, and some historians might argue that political parties and presidential politics contributed to the advent of the Civil War. The nominating conventions of both the Republican and the Democratic parties, from 1876 to beyond World War I, present a neat block for a study of practices of party professionals, leaders, or bosses, which can help today in assessing the best path for additional reform or refinement in our nominating process.

For almost fifty years, from Ulysses S. Grant's last term to Warren G. Harding's election, both parties experienced internal upheavals and demands for reform in delegate selection and convention voting. The party professionals and bosses were active at the beginning of that period and still dominant at the end of the period. They lost as often as they won, often canceled out one another, withstood the takeover or attack by both liberal and conservative forces, survived third-party defections, endured William Jennings Bryan in one party and adjusted partially to Teddy Roosevelt in the other, and overall and collectively participated in a remarkable period of presidential leadership.

The conventions were surprisingly open. Neither party had a central group of willful men conspiring in back rooms to manipulate the party and the presidency to their selfish and crooked purposes. Oh, plenty were selfish and crooked, but there were also numerous party participants who saw politics as an exciting duty. Generally there were several, sometimes many, groups of men opposing one another, struggling for the power and purposes of the presidency.

Nothing much has really changed. Today we still have coteries of men, and now women, struggling to manipulate delegations for the power and purposes of the presidency. How those people arrived in such a position of leadership and power—how they became "bosses"—is the factor that is different. How well they perform for the nation remains the crucial concern.

In 1876 President Grant was completing has second term with a somewhat tarnished administration. Long out of power, the Democrats were nursing near-mortal wounds. In 1872 they had weakly endorsed Horace Greeley, the candidate nominated by the Liberal Republicans, a group that had splintered that year from the regular Republican party. Both the Democratic and the Republican parties had reasons to be seeking a fresh start.

Parenthetically, of that Liberal Republican party nomination, William Gillette noted,

How then could the convention have nominated the worst possible candidate? Perhaps the answer is that political amateurs assembled to run a national convention of a party without organization represented by delegates without constituencies make political decisions ineffectively. . . . Their collective failure was to hold a convention too open and too fluid to make much sense or serve much purpose. It was spring madness combined with peculiar politics and strange enthusiasm. [1]

That comment is disturbingly close to what some observers have said about some recent conventions.

The 1876 Republican Convention was the sixth held by that political coalition, which had been organized in 1854. The party had given previous nominations to John C. Fremont, Abraham Lincoln, and Grant. President Grant's administration had been marked by scandals and bad management. The Democrats, who actually had no real Democratic candidate in 1872, had made a miraculous return from death, gaining control of both houses of the Congress and a number of statehouses in 1874.

President Grant still enjoyed widespread personal loyalty because of his hero status, and he was willing to break George Washington's admonition and run for a third term. Fortunately for the country, a number of leading Republicans ("bosses" they might be called, certainly "party pros") read the attitudes of their party constituencies and the public and held ambitions not attainable through Grant. Those men would have none of Grant's third-term talk.

One such person was the leader of the congressional group known as the Half-Breeds, those congressional Republicans who generally restrained or opposed the president. He was James G. Blaine of Maine, and he had been Speaker of the House of Representatives until the Democrats had taken control in 1874. He had accumulated a wide following across the country, among Republican leaders and party workers, with whom he had been associated in various situations, and he was recognized as the leading contender for the presidency. Republican conventions in state after state were pledging to support him and electing as delegates men who were favorable toward him.

There were others determined to defeat Blaine, and (to simplify the explanation) these were the Grant loyalists, the Stalwarts led by Senator Roscoe Conkling of New York—who was also the Republican boss of New York—and Senator O. P. Morton of Indiana—noted for his extreme anti-South positions ("waving the bloody flag" it was called). Both men were candidates, and both had President Grant's blessing; both were primarily interested in stopping Blaine, and both perhaps hoped that a deadlocked convention would renominate Grant.

Then there were those men who had their own ambitions to be president. Benjamin Bristow of Kentucky was one. He had been a part of the Grant administration but had earned Grant's enmity and the public's appreciation when, as secretary of the treasury, he had exposed the Whiskey Ring. His principal support came from the Liberal Republicans, led by the Republican boss of Missouri. This faction, which had broken away in a separate convention to nominate and run Horace Greeley, had now returned to the Republican party and hoped to liberalize from within. Another with his own ambitions was Governor Rutherford B. Hayes of Ohio, with support primarily from Ohio.

Then there were those leaders, or bosses, like Donald Cameron of Pennsylvania. He was probably not guided by professed lofty goals like the liberals nor motivated by rivalry, ambition, or hatred like Conkling; he was simply willing to trade with the winner for Pennsylvania's, and his, advantage. Cameron had a favorite son candidate, Governor John Hartranft of Pennsylvania.

In all accuracy the 1876 convention could be called an open convention. It was not dominated by the sitting president nor by any coalition of party leaders. But plenty of bosses and subbosses were there, and the two most powerful groupings were squared off for a death struggle.

Blaine almost won. Rutherford B. Hayes was nominated on the seventh ballot. It is worth remembering that the Republicans have never used the two-thirds rule for nomination (which the Democrats bound themselves with until 1936); Blaine was stopped just short of a simple majority. It is also worth noting that this Republican Convention reaffirmed that party's rule that outlawed the binding of delegates by a unit rule, whereas the Democrats clung in some degree to that "bosses' tool" until their 1980 convention.

In the delegates' deliberation at the convention, something we seldom see today, Blaine lost an almost unbeatable lead for several reasons. He was suspected of having received some improper payment from the railroads, and shortly before the convention he had made a ringing anti-South speech to gain favor with the more militant unionists, a move he apparently felt necessary because he had not served in the military. "It was a dishonest speech and a base appeal to cheap emotions, but it was enormously effective. . . . The speech shattered his name for magnanimous statemanship, but it made Blaine a partisan of the first order and, as he well knew, partisanship, not magnanimity, is the high road to the White House."[2] His strategy backfired. Largely because of the image that speech projected, the liberals would not support him, when their support was all he needed. His manager also turned down a deal with Donald Cameron, who offered Hartranft's votes in exchange for a cabinet position for a Pennsylvanian, a modest price. The deal was rejected because Blaine's manager thought Blaine had the nomination won.

It was not just a deliberative convention that defeated Blaine. Grant's people were determined. The last chance that Morton and Conkling had to stop Blaine was to shift their votes to someone else, and Rutherford B. Hayes was just standing there, available. He was not beholden to Conkling, then or later. Morton and Conkling managed to shift to Hayes just in time not to get themselves a president, but to defeat Blaine.

Actually Hayes had been doing more than just standing there. The liberals also came to Hayes from Bristow because the Hayes managers worked out a deal with the Bristow managers before the first ballot whereby the latter's support would go to Hayes if Bristow began to falter in the balloting. There was on the part of Bristow's managers a desire to defeat Blaine, but the sweetener for the liberals and the Bristow bosses was a promise by the Hayes managers to appoint to the Supreme Court the chairman of the Bristow Kentucky delegation and Bristow's law partner, John Marshall Harlan.[3]

The 1876 Republican Convention could also be considered an open convention because a lot of independent delegates were a part of it. But it was essentially a bosses' convention, with bosses arrayed against one another. There was deliberation in the sense that the die was not cast with the opening gavel. Most of the delegates were party workers, so the convention was not open in the sense that any citizen could have been a delegate. Some delegates came from districts in which there were few Republicans other than the delegate himself, notably in the South. The delegates, all of them, wanted a winner. They divided on opinion, but they united finally after a spirited convention.

The resurrected Democrats in 1876 carried on a campaign and conducted a convention in an open manner without deals and trading by bosses. Out of power since before the Civil War, the Democrats felt that victory was at hand. As Governor Samuel J. Tilden of New York expressed it in his letter of acceptance of the presidential nomination (nominees did not show up to accept the nomination until Franklin Roosevelt set the precedent in 1932), Tilden had been "educated in the belief that it is the first duty of a citizen of the Republic to take his fair allotment of care and trouble in public affairs, [and] I have for forty years as a private citizen fulfilled that duty."[4] He had become the "reform governor," having already sent Boss Tweed to the penitentiary, and he had assumed leadership of the New York Democratic party.

Tilden had received wide recognition for his reform successes, and he set out methodically to translate that recognition into delegate votes. He conducted what Herbert Eaton has called the first "modern" campaign for the nomination.[5] He advertised in 1,200 newspapers, sent them a series of articles about himself, prepared and distributed thoughtful articles on relevant subjects, surveyed commencement addresses and Fourth of July speeches to learn the temper of the nation (which he found to be reform-minded), and by the time the convention met he was all but assured the nomination. Delegates, of course, were selected by state conventions in a variety of ways.

Since the two-thirds rule applied, any opposition was serious, and Tilden, a "hard money" man, was opposed by a candidate with a "greenback" point of view, a position popular in the West. The convention was held in St. Louis. Tilden, who discreetly was not present at the convention, had prepared the platform, and the first confrontation was on the money plank. Tilden had made it clear he would not run if the soft money position were taken by the party, and he won two to one after riotous conduct and debate. "The Convention was in bedlam, but the Tilden steamroller moved on."[6] Tilden was loudly opposed by the Tammany Hall faction, but except for adding to the unruliness, this opposition was advantageous for a reform candidate, and, besides, the unit rule locked in, or out, that faction's votes as New York delegates.

There were five other candidates, including the greenback candidate who had learned of his fate when the platform was adopted. On the first ballot Tilden received 54 percent of the vote. On the second ballot he passed the necessary two-thirds mark. The vice-presidential candidate selected was the greenback candidate, Senator Thomas H. Hendricks of Indiana, apparently selected not because of any deal but in a spirit of unity for the party, made unanimous by a "brotherhood speech" by the boss of Tammany.

Samuel J. Tilden had won the nomination because of a good record, carefully explained, and superior organization. He probably would have become one of our better presidents. The results of the election count between Tilden and Hayes are well known, or should be, for it can still be contended that Tilden won the presidency.[7]

In 1880 Hayes was not a candidate, having announced early that he would not stand for reelection. Conkling was back, this time to fight for the nomination for a third term for the willing Ulysses S. Grant. Grant was still an extremely popular public hero. As boss of New York, Conkling had overrun the usual practice that permitted district conventions to instruct their delegates, and at the state convention he had forced a resolution that purported to pledge all New York delegates to Grant.

Senator John Sherman of Ohio, brother of the general, had been a key figure in the nomination of Hayes and was the administration's candidate. President Hayes, however, had little influence to offer. James G. Blaine, still with wide support, was back and was the leading anti-Grant candidate.

There were candidates from Vermont, Illinois, and Minnesota, and John Sherman had a dark horse lurking in his own corral, Congressman James A. Garfield of Ohio. Sherman took care of that competition by pressuring Garfield to stand aside, Sherman promising to swing his votes to Garfield if Sherman failed. He also talked Garfield into being his campaign manager, which perhaps was a fatal mistake for Sherman. Garfield's private position was that he did not seek the nomination, but was available. The visibility he attained as Sherman's manager made Garfield even more available.

The bosses of the various delegations were mostly arrayed for Grant or Blaine, but there were always enough bosses to go around so Garfield himself was favored by a few who were working and ready. One, a Philadelphia banker, advised Garfield that he would work for Garfield while Garfield worked for Sherman, with the aim of defeating Grant with one or the other. Because the Blaine people had contested for Ohio delegates in Sherman's home state, and had even won a few, there was little chance of Sherman's key leaders going to Blaine, even to stop Grant.

The boss of Illinois, John A. Logan, who with the likes of Conkling wanted to return to power with Grant, railroaded a new delegate selection process through the Illinois Republican Convention, which he controlled. The authority of district delegates to the state convention to name national delegates was removed, and that authority was given to a committee appointed by Logan. This kind of "bossism" illustrates how the bosses earned a bad name, a reputation probably not deserved by the vast majority of party leaders struggling for the power and purposes of the presidency.

The key boss strategy of the Grant forces was to impose the unit rule on the convention. To achieve this, they would use the chairman of the National Republican Committee, our old friend Donald Cameron, the boss of Pennsylvania who had been unable to strike a deal with Blaine in 1876 and who was now a stalwart Grant supporter. As party chairman, Cameron would preside over the convention during the election of the temporary chairman, and he would rule that the unit rule applied for that election. Having elected a favorable temporary chairman, that person in turn would rule that the unit rule applied for the credentials questions and the adoption of rules that had been drafted to apply the unit rule to the nominating procedures. Neatly, as they counted the votes, this procedure would assure Grant's nomination.

The bosses did not prevail. The Republican National Committee, itself with an anti-Grant majority, moved that there would be no unit rule in the convention, but Cameron refused to entertain the motion, maintaining that the committee did not have such authority and that the issue had to be decided by the convention. After a day's standoff, the anti-Grant committee members threatened to oust Cameron. The Grant forces then attempted to pressure the sergeant-at-arms not to recognize a new party chairman, but he declined, and there ended the bosses' takeover for Grant. In proper time, with a neutral chairman, the convention voted against the unit rule, as the Republican party always had.

It was a bitter convention. Conkling proposed a loyalty pledge early, and when three West Virginia delegates voted against it, he moved they be expelled. James A. Garfield made a spirited rebuttal. "We come here as Republicans, . . .

and as one of our rights, we can vote on every resolution 'aye' or 'no.' We are responsible for those votes to our constituents, and to them alone."[8] Conkling withdrew his motion. But the discussion meant more exposure for Garfield, and a very sound principle of delegate participation was reaffirmed by the Republican party. Conkling nominated Grant, to the tumultuous cheering of the Grant delegates and the galleries. Garfield made a great nomination speech for Sherman, barely mentioning his name.

The unit rule, it was calculated, would have put Grant within 21 votes of a majority. With delegates exercising their independent judgment, he was some 75 short, and he stayed that short for thirty-three ballots. Blaine stayed about 100 votes short. Conkling's actions had solidified the opposition. Sherman would not release his 90-plus votes to either Blaine or Grant. There were three other candidates.

Wharton Barker of Philadelphia, Garfield's unauthorized but effective manager, started the switch on the thirty-fourth ballot, and Garfield received only 17 votes. Garfield rose to challenge the right of anyone to vote for him without his approval. He was ruled out of order by the chairman. On the thirty-fifth ballot Grant held, Blaine slipped a little, Sherman held, and Garfield received 50 votes.

On the thirty-sixth ballot, New York and the Grant people held firm and gave Grant his 306 votes, only 2 more than he had received on the first ballot. Blaine got 42 stubborn votes, Garfield voted for Sherman, and 399 other delegates voted for Garfield.[9]

Chester A. Arthur, recently removed by President Hayes from his Port of New York position for alleged corruption, maybe without due cause, was too hastily selected by the Garfield managers for the vice-presidential position. In not much more than a year Garfield had been assassinated, and Arthur was president.

Conventions were becoming a tradition. Bosses were

bosses, and the party convention was their arena, but they never quite directed the affair.

Notes

1. William Gillette, "Election of 1872," in *History of American Presidential Elections*, vol. 2, *1848–1896*, ed. Arthur M. Schlesinger, Jr. (New York: Chelsea House Publishers, 1971), p. 1315.

2. Herbert Eaton, *Presidential Timber: A History of Nominating Conventions, 1869–1960* (New York: Free Press of Glencoe, 1964), p. 45.

3. Ibid., p. 55.

4. "Acceptance letter of Governor Samuel J. Tilden," July 31, 1876, in *History of American Presidential Elections*, vol. 2, *1848–1896*, p. 1453.

5. Eaton, *Presidential Timber*, p. 61.

6. Ibid., p. 64.

7. For an account of the Tilden-Hayes dispute, see Eugene H. Roseboom, *A History of Presidential Elections*, 3d ed. (London: Macmillan Company, 1970), pp. 236–249.

8. Ibid., pp. 74–75.

9. Ibid., p. 84.

5

Bosses and
Upset Applecarts

There were bosses and bosses, and certainly the memory of Mark Hanna of Ohio is in the image of a boss. In the decade after Garfield's assassination Chester Arthur had served out the term, James G. Blaine had finally received the nomination, the Republicans had been defeated by Grover Cleveland, and in turn they had nominated Benjamin Harrison, who beat Cleveland. During this period a substantial businessman, Mark Hanna, had been developing political power in Ohio. He had played a leading part, using some questionable tactics, in the unsuccessful campaigns to nominate John Sherman.

In 1892 Hanna was on hand at the Republican Convention and grooming William McKinley, Jr., former governor of Ohio and then secretary of the treasury. McKinley was a member of the president's cabinet and was properly loyal. President Benjamin Harrison was renominated, to be soundly defeated by Grover Cleveland, but McKinley, whose name was not placed in nomination, got one-third as many votes as Harrison and the same number received by Blaine. Hanna was pleased, retired from business in 1895, and by 1896 was prepared to gain the nomination for McKinley.

It was a time of the Cleveland Panic, and the political parties were sharply divided over silver, the tariff, and the general effects of the depression. Free silver was the symbol of the opposition. In the preconvention period, Hanna's campaign for McKinley was against the bosses, and indeed there were many bosses supporting other candidates and willing to trade. By the time of the convention Hanna had the nomination sewed up and was dictating the terms of the platform.

The most dramatic moment was the defeat of a substitute free-silver plank, which caused the senators from Colorado, Utah, and Montana and some of their delegations to withdraw, that is, bolt the party. "Mark Hanna could be heard shouting in fury, 'Go, Go.' "[1] A Democrat, the editor of an Omaha paper, was watching. His name was William Jennings Bryan. Later that season he was to overwhelm the Democratic party and gain the nomination on a silver platform.

Hanna had no trouble getting McKinley elected, McKinley had no trouble serving well enough to assure himself the renomination, and in 1900 he was the unanimous choice of the delegates. Hanna's trouble was with the bosses—the other bosses—and especially the boss of New York. That boss wanted Governor Theodore Roosevelt out of New York and was scheming to get him the vice-presidential nomination (Vice-President Garret A. Hobart had died). Hanna was screaming, "Don't any of you realize that there's only one life between that madman and the Presidency?"[2] President McKinley refused to take sides. The principal bosses, Thomas Platt of New York and Matthew Quay of Pennsylvania, had scores to settle with Hanna in addition to Platt's determination to relegate Roosevelt to obscurity outside of New York.

Hanna's troubles were not just with the bosses, but also with Roosevelt's personal appeal to the youthful and frontier spirit of the nation. He was the romantic Roughrider. The names of numerous other possibilities, distinguished senators and cabinet members, were trotted out by Hanna but to no avail, since they did not have matching appeal and since the president wouldn't help his old mentor by endorsing anyone.

Roosevelt was overwhelmingly supported by the delegates who refused to be influenced by the bosses. That they might have been manipulated by Platt is another question. Disturbed by suggestions that he was the bosses' candidate, Roosevelt, still protesting candidacy, denounced Platt at the convention and thus added to the luster of his hero's crown. Platt smiled, well satisfied.

In short order an assassin's bullet had made Roosevelt president, and the strongest boss of the era had been powerless to prevent that situation. Whether Roosevelt could have been nominated for president had he remained vice-president cannot be answered. No vice-president had been nominated for the presidency since Martin Van Buren in 1836, and only Nixon and Humphrey have been in this century.

For 1904 the only strong, visible opponent to Roosevelt's renomination was Senator Mark Hanna (U.S. senators were elected by state legislatures until 1912), who was showing signs of willingness to carry the conservative banner when he died in 1903. It would have been some convention!

Roosevelt, renominated and reelected, left the presidency to William Howard Taft in 1909 but returned in 1912. Motivated by a combination of dissatisfaction with President Taft and continuing burning personal ambition, Roosevelt was determined to kick over the applecart of the Republican party. He challenged the bosses, who supported Taft's renomination, and was decisively defeated in the 1912 Republican Convention. His response was to start a third party,[3] which assured Taft's defeat, but it disintegrated the next year when it was no longer of any use to Teddy Roosevelt.

> When the convention came together it was predicted almost or quite universally by the newspaper correspondents in attendance that Taft's nomination had been assured by the action of the

National Committee, since the "Steam Roller" would pursue its course as inflexibly in the convention as it had in the committee. This prediction was fulfilled literally. [4]

At the conclusion of the committee's work, it was announced officially that 92 contests had been investigated and decided; there had been no roll-calls in 74 decisions; roll-calls in 16; unanimous vote in 4, and 2 contests had been abandoned. The net result was that 233 of the contested delegates were given to Taft and 6 to Roosevelt. The daily records of the proceedings of the committee were published in the newspapers of the country under such head-lines as the "Steam Roller Continues Its Work." [5]

"What do you fellows intend to do?" [David W.] Mulvane was asked. "You know you surely can't elect Taft."

To which Mulvane is said to have responded:

"We can't elect Taft, but we are going to hold on to this organization, and when we get back four years from now we will have it and not those d— insurgents." [6]

Bosses could be bosses, especially when they were organized behind a sitting president.

Notes

1. Herbert Eaton, *Presidential Timber: A History of Nominating Conventions, 1869–1960* (New York: Free Press of Glencoe, 1964), p. 153.

2. Ibid., p. 184.

3. It is difficult to avoid the temptation to discuss third-party excursions, but they are beyond the purpose of this book. That they have been influential as a threat in the nominating process cannot be denied. They also have been an indication that the principal parties have not been affording an adequate openness for all elements of society to feel they have received a full hearing. Often they have been no more significant than a display of some personal ambition. For the most interesting and by far the most significant third-party movement, see Lawrence

Goodwyn, *Democratic Promise: The Populist Moment in America* (New York: Oxford University Press, 1976).

4. Joseph Bucklin Bishop, *Presidential Nominations and Elections* (New York: Charles Scribner's Sons, 1916), p. 107.

5. Ibid., p. 105.

6. Ibid.

6

The Deliberative Convention

No candidate for the presidential nomination has ever risen so high to fall so far as a certain man from Missouri who might have been president. At the Democratic National Convention he led the voting for the first twenty-nine ballots, achieving a clear majority for twenty ballots. Prior to the convention he had entered nine of the twelve presidential primaries and won five, including substantial victories in California and Illinois, while losing one to the favorite son in Ohio. His chief opponent technically defeated him in one primary and straight out in only Oregon and Wisconsin.[1] With all this support, he did not gain the nomination.

He would have been the Democratic nominee and probably the president, since Teddy Roosevelt had split from the Republicans that year, had the rules of his convention been the same as those of the Republican party—or had the rules of the Democratic party of today been in effect.

The year was 1912. The loser, who seemed to have won it all the way, was Champ Clark of Missouri. Instead, the Democrats nominated Woodrow Wilson on the forty-sixth ballot. The drama of that convention can be used to argue that the two-thirds rule was unfair, undemocratic, and thwarted the will of the electorate. The same drama can also be summoned up to argue that the two-thirds rule forced deliberation and more careful and thoughtful consideration by the delegates and that, accordingly, on the final count wisdom and clear thinking triumphed, and the better man was nominated.

Most historians assume that Wilson made a better president than Clark would have made, although that conclusion is subjective. That Wilson became president because of the delays and the enforced consideration and reconsideration by the delegates cannot be denied. In the beginning, conventions were viewed as occasions for party leaders and delegates to come together to seek out the best man for the presidency. The nomination of Woodrow Wilson seemed to justify this hope and to make the case for the two-thirds rule.

After the tenth ballot when Clark received a clear majority of the convention, the tumult and the shouting arose from the Clark supporters, for "not in sixty-eight years, had a candidate won a majority and failed to go on to the required two-thirds."[2] Did the repeated balloting bring a deliberative element into the nominating process?

> The badly shaken Wilson managers quickly gathered on the platform for consultation. Agreeing on a plan of action, A. Mitchell Palmer, the floor leader, McAdoo, . . . Henry Morgenthau . . . and the other Wilson leaders scurried about the hall. Ignoring the tumultuous demonstration blaring in their ears, they persuaded the Underwood leaders, who were considering giving up, to stand fast. If they would hold their lines, they were told, and Wilson later failed nomination, his votes would go to Underwood.[3]

The Wilson managers also, without Wilson's knowledge, traded the vice-presidency for 31 Indiana votes. Calm deliberation?

And listen to the convention discussion of the issues. William Jennings Bryan, three times the Democratic nominee, "arose to introduce a resolution. 'As proof of our fidelity to the people, we hereby declare ourselves opposed to any candidate for president who is the representative of or under obligation to J. Pierpont Morgan, Thomas Fortune Ryan, August Belmont, or any other member of the privilege-hunting and favor-seeking class.' " The resolution went on to "demand the withdrawal from the convention of any delegate or delegates constituting or representing" such interests.[4] As for deliberate debate of that issue, "A Virginia delegate leaped onto the platform and shook his fist in Bryan's face but became completely hysterical and was led away by his friends."[5]

Regarding an examination of the qualifications of the candidates, Bryan took the floor to announce on the thirteenth ballot that Nebraska Clark supporters, of which he was one, "will not participate in the nomination of any man whose nomination depends upon the vote of the New York delegation." Therefore they would withhold their support from Clark.[6]

Did the two-thirds vote requirement add a useful dimension that is now lacking? The place of Woodrow Wilson in American history is certainly a direct result of the two-thirds rule. The only other time the front-runner had a clear majority and did not run on victoriously to the finish line was in 1844 when James K. Polk appeared for the first time on the eighth ballot after Martin Van Buren, attempting a comeback, had had 55 percent of the delegates on the first ballot with six other candidates receiving votes. That was a unique situation: Polk having entered the convention as a mere vice-presidential candidate was finally acceptable to all. Polk, too, became president as a result of the two-thirds rule.

The two-thirds rule plagued Franklin D. Roosevelt in 1932, and it was changed by his command in 1936 so that only a simple majority is required, and that is how the rule stands today. The Republican party never adopted a two-thirds rule, although attempts were made to do so.

The questions remain, Is the convention deliberative enough? Can it indeed be deliberative? How did the two-thirds rule affect nominations until 1936, and what would have been the convention decisions if the rule had not been abolished?

The Democrats nominated Horace Greeley on the first ballot in 1872, Samuel J. Tilden on the second ballot in 1876, Winfield Scott Hancock on the second ballot in 1880, and Grover Cleveland on the second ballot in 1884, by acclamation in 1888, and on the first ballot in 1892.

William Jennings Bryan took the nomination in 1896 on the fifth ballot, having started in second place, and there is no doubt that opinions formed and decisions made by the delegates in convention moved them to support Bryan. He was nominated on the first ballot four years later. In 1904 Bryan opposed Alton B. Parker, giving typical Bryan obtuse support to William Randolph Hearst. In spite of Bryan, Parker received votes that put him only 9 short of two-thirds on the first ballot, with shifts making a second ballot unnecessary. In 1908 Bryan went after the nomination again and got it on the first ballot with very little opposition. Thus it was not until 1912 that the two-thirds rule began to cause mischief or confer benefits or both.

In 1916 Woodrow Wilson was renominated on the first ballot. In 1920 there were more than twenty Democratic candidates at the starting line, and forty-four ballots later James M. Cox was nominated. He had run third behind William G. McAdoo and A. Mitchell Palmer until the last few ballots, and no one received even a simple majority until the next to last ballot. (Franklin D. Roosevelt was nominated for the vice-presidency.)

The 1924 Democratic nominee, John W. Davis, began in ninth place with 31 votes (there were 1,098 delegate votes and seventeen candidates), crept up to over 100, and dropped back by some 30 to 50 votes after 38 ballots. He stayed there behind William G. McAdoo, who led all the way until the

100th ballot, and Alfred E. Smith, who ran second. Davis was nominated on the 103rd ballot. No candidate ever had a simple majority until the last ballot. Whatever deliberation might have benefited the body politic, it was more than offset by the ordeal and the injury of the deadlocks.

In 1928 Al Smith received 914 votes out of 1,100, and transfers quickly made the nomination almost unanimous. It was the third time he had been a serious contender, and he was well known. He was nominated by Franklin D. Roosevelt, as he had been in 1924. There was not much point in discussion and deliberation. Delegates from twenty states seconded his nomination, and he received votes from forty-three of the forty-eight states on the first roll call.

In 1932 it took four ballots for Franklin Roosevelt to move from 666 votes, a clear majority, to 945, well beyond the two-thirds mark. There were 1,154 delegate votes that year. His principal opposition was Al Smith, making one last try. John Nance Garner of Texas was potentially a threat, as was the eminent Newton D. Baker of Ohio. There were the makings of another 1924 donnybrook, but the leaders, except for the Smith crowd, had no stomach for it. Had it not been for the two-thirds rule, it would not have been necessary to go beyond the first ballot. That was the last time the two-thirds rule, which had given the country President Polk and President Wilson, was used.

Could John Kennedy have received two-thirds of the vote in Los Angeles? He got 53 percent, had powerful opposition from Lyndon Johnson and Stuart Symington, and Adlai Stevenson was eager in the wings. Hubert Humphrey received two-thirds of the votes on the first ballot in Chicago. In 1972 could George McGovern, with 57 percent of the delegates, have maintained his strength after the first ballot, or would the convention delegates have looked again at Edmund Muskie, or attached to Henry Jackson, or called back Hubert Humphrey? Could Wallace, with 12.5 percent of the first ballot, finally have blocked McGovern and cut a deal with someone else?

Is a convention a likely place for deliberation, for careful examination of the candidates and their capacities? We need this reflective element somewhere in the presidential process, but we are unlikely to attain it by trying to build it into the convention proceedings. Although it is never too late to reflect and reexamine, the pitch of emotional excitement, the dynamics of ambitious people, the size of the stakes, and the immediacy of every move make it doubtful that there will be calm discussion, if any discussion at all, at a national political convention.

Perhaps it is inevitable that the party conventions in the United States must be circus grounds with acrobatic performers providing light television entertainment for a casual public. Or is there some chance we might make our conventions places of enlightenment and education, with citizens gathered together to select with wisdom and care the best leader possible for a great nation on whom the rest of the world is so dependent for so much? Hardly, as the procedures and rules now stand.

Is it possible that conventions have outlived their usefulness? To put an alternative question, was the two-thirds rule abandoned without due consideration for its advantages in preventing hurried and possibly ill-advised nominations? Would it be well to consider a two-thirds rule for the first five ballots—or even for the first ballot only?

Notes

1. James W. Davis, *Presidential Primaries: Road to the White House* (New York: Thomas Y. Crowell Company, 1967), p. 279.
2. Herbert Eaton, *Presidential Timber: A History of Nominating Conventions, 1869–1960* (New York: Free Press of Glencoe, 1964), p. 238.
3. Ibid., pp. 238–239.
4. Ibid., pp. 236–237. (August Belmont was himself a delegate.)
5. Ibid., p. 237.
6. Ibid., p. 240.

7

Representative Delegates

What happened finally to the California delegation's vote in the 1960 Democratic Convention may well be the most important lesson for today to come out of that exciting political year. It proved that delegates can think for themselves.

Except for the primary maze (the word "system" will not do), it is likely that John F. Kennedy, George McGovern, and Jimmy Carter would not have been nominated. Wendell Willkie might have received his second nomination except for the primaries. Ronald Reagan almost took the 1976 nomination away from President Gerald Ford because of them. Edmund Muskie was knocked out of the Democratic nomination in 1972 because of a bad showing, or a perceived bad showing, in the primaries. Hubert Humphrey had to do well in the 1972 primaries, which he did not, as distinguished from his successful nomination campaign in 1968, which was unique enough to make primaries unimportant for him.

John Kennedy used the primary series to show the leaders, the voting public, and the active participating Democrats that he was electable. He did not use the primaries to get nominated as, say, Estes Kefauver had tried to do. Kennedy sought, and won, the nomination by going after the party leadership just as surely as Franklin Roosevelt had in the early thirties. It was a campaign of the jet-prop age, compared to Jim Farley's campaign in the diesel-locomotive age. Larry O'Brien and Bobby Kennedy were doing the same thing Farley had done, except that the style, like everything else in America, had become faster and more frantic.

Winning primaries alone would not have nominated Kennedy, any more than winning them could nominate Kefauver. Kefauver had made them more important, indeed essential for a relatively unknown person, but Kefauver did not go after the leaders. Primaries were significant in 1960, but they were not yet decisive.

John Kennedy was not known in 1959, he was a first-term senator who had not made much of a congressional mark, but he was an unusually attractive, talented, and intelligent man who would, as it turned out, make a good president. He was adequately ambitious and from a family of intense ambition. He could not have won as Franklin Roosevelt won. Roosevelt ran on a distinguished record, was widely known and admired, and had a name already recognized in presidential politics. John Kennedy needed much more as he set out in quest of the presidency. He needed to prove he was a winner, he needed to prove his charm was based on intelligence, he needed to exhibit "presidential characteristics." He needed the primaries. Particularly as a Roman Catholic and as a relatively young man, he needed a proving ground. The primaries would give him that proof, without having to establish a Roosevelt-like record. Primaries, he judged, would convince the bosses if he could bring off enough wins at the right times.

Kennedy's primary course was carefully calculated. His financing and budget were adequate. His appeal in person and on the platform was irresistible. His, or his father's, connections with important media opinion-shapers were firm. If he lost a single crucial primary battle he would be mortally wounded, and he could not hope to win without a trail of victories. He also knew that victories would not be enough. He would have to convince the governors of Pennsylvania, New Jersey, and elsewhere, the satraps of New York, the New England senators, party leadership in the South, and Democrats generally everywhere that he was the leader who had arrived, fresh and strong and exuberant, "born in this century," ready to "go forth to lead the land we love."[1]

Although it had been unnecessary, and perhaps inappropriate and in poor taste, for Franklin Roosevelt to campaign personally across the land, the 1960s demanded that the candidate appear everywhere and all at once. The changing importance of the primaries demanded a handshaking campaign. It was becoming like a sheriff's race nationwide, except no candidates for sheriff ever looked as uniformly silly as the Democratic leaders looked campaigning in Florida in 1972 for the presidency of the United States.

Kennedy's victory in the West Virginia primary was crucial. He "proved to the skeptical uncommitted big-city Democratic leaders—the power bloc that determines who will be the party nominee—that he was the type of vote-getting candidate needed to sweep the party to victory in November."[2] It laid to rest the "Pope issue," since there were almost no Catholics in West Virginia. It was his third significant victory, and it caused Hubert Humphrey to withdraw from the race. (But isn't there something wrong with a system that compels a distinguished leader to withdraw before there is time for the vast majority of the voters to look him over and have their say?) Johnson, Symington, and Stevenson did not withdraw. They were in contention in Los Angeles, but then they had not chosen to go the primary route. Kennedy had already won solidly in New Hampshire and adequately in Humphrey's backyard, Wisconsin, and he was on his way. West Virginia was a turning point, but Kennedy still needed to win the party leadership. The primaries would only help establish consensus; real consensus had to come through the party leaders.

Even during the last hours at the convention in Los Angeles Kennedy needed to dash from hotel to hotel to appear before delegations to gain their support or to hold his support steady. This was a useful exercise, some of it needless but of help in giving the delegates an opportunity to see and question the candidate. This exercise might be seen as the delegates' consideration of issues, examination of the candidates, and deliberation, to a degree far less than would be desirable but far more genuine than the deliberation and consideration that went on at Wilson's convention in 1912 or Franklin Roosevelt's in 1932—or later at George McGovern's, Barry Goldwater's, or Jimmy Carter's. Progress was being made in the nominating process. More people voted and more were involved in delegate selection. There was some deliberation and thoughtful consideration by the delegates in convention.

Lyndon Johnson also made the rounds in 1960, frequently presented and sponsored by the U.S. senator from the state he was greeting, and he picked up some added support. Stuart Symington, generally unknown by the delegates, made an excellent impression with his visits, and doubtless he would have been an attractive second choice for both Johnson and Kennedy supporters had the balloting gone beyond one roll call. That did not happen because there was no two-thirds rule, and the primaries had given Kennedy an advantage that turned out to be insurmountable. The bosses were still on hand, but Kennedy had used the primaries to get to the bosses, to reassure the politically concerned party workers.

That was the last truly contested Democratic Convention before the new rules and before the number of delegates was almost doubled. It was the first in which primaries played a crucial and winning part and the last in which the presence of bosses forced deliberation to achieve consensus. If the Democrats did so well in 1960, why did they change their rules so drastically? If the rules needed changing for other reasons, did the Democrats retain or somehow lose the elements that made 1960 successful?

In 1960 there were sixteen states in which Democratic primaries were held. In 1980 there were thirty-two Democratic state primaries, plus the District of Columbia and Puerto Rico. There were 1,521 delegates to be selected for Kennedy's convention, and delegates were selected by direct vote, by conventions, by district caucuses, by appointment or the equivalent of appointment, or by a combination of those methods. In 1980 the Democrats had 3,331 convention delegates, all slated and selected under the new rules.

Blacks were excluded as delegates in a few states and largely ignored in many others in 1960, and caucuses were often private affairs. Caucuses are now open and advertised. Participants are sought after because of affirmative action, and many new rules prevent manipulation and stacking of the cards by party leaders.

In 1960, those people who ran for delegate posts wanted to run, and they won if they managed to get enough votes or the nod of the key figures, whatever was required in the respective bailiwicks. In 1980 they won if they were on a ticket allotted to a presidential candidate to whom they were pledged, if they were approved by the candidate and if the candidate got enough caucus or primary votes to carry them with him.

Most delegates were not legally pledged in advance of the 1960 convention, but in 1976 and 1980 almost all delegates were pledged in advance. This was the substantial difference. The delegate in 1960 generally had much more independence and freedom in voting than the average delegate in 1976 and 1980.

There were more than fifty variations in the method of delegate selection in 1960. In 1980 much more uniformity was demanded by the rules, but as Richard Stearns pointed out, "There aren't more than 100 people in the country who fully understand the rules of the Democratic Party as we've written them now."[3]

If our desire is to shape a presidential nominating process that earns credibility and is representative, open, participatory, fair, deliberative, thoughtful, and designed to attract and select the best possible leader for our nation—a leader who can draw together a popular consensus, both to win and to govern—we need to dissect the system of delegate selection and examine the parts. Then, we might seek simpler and more understandable rules that permit us to obtain a process with the characteristics we have set. There are several crucial questions, the most important being, Are delegates who are not instructed, as was generally the case in 1960, less representative than those who arrive at the convention with a binding pledge to vote for a particular candidate?

Delegates that numerous organizations send to conventions, which to some degree are legislative bodies, are generally there to be representative of the local body or constituency that sent them. This representation is fairly easy when the local body is a civic club or an American Legion post. If there is an issue the local unit wants to vote a particular way, the group is ordinarily small and homogeneous in thought, and it is fairly simple for the delegate to know how to vote. Giving instructions is more complicated when the delegate is a congressman representing a congressional district full of a variety of people and interests or a city alderman representing a ward. He or she cannot be reasonably instructed on every important issue, and except in a most unusual situation such a representative is expected to represent voters and nonvoters to the best of his or her own judgment. Most conscientious representatives take into account the desires of the constituency and their own view of the broader society they also represent as members of the governing body. Such representatives can be and frequently are bombarded by their constituents when some issue of interest is up for a vote.

Is a political convention analogous to Congress? Should delegates be elected to exercise individual judgment on matters of platform, credentials, rules, and even candidates? Are delegates elected because of their individual character and ability, with trust reposed in them to represent the district with honor and intelligence? Do the new rules make convention delegates merely high-powered, honorific messengers? The question is, What do we want them to be?

When Woodrow Wilson, Franklin Roosevelt, Adlai Stevenson, Thomas E. Dewey, and Dwight D. Eisenhower were nominated, the delegates were recognizable individuals selected because of party activity or public position. Generally these delegates enjoyed the confidence and trust of the constituencies from which they were chosen. They had a sense of the political climate and attitudes, and they were looking for a presidential candidate satisfactory to the people in their respective home districts. Frequently delegate selection was decidedly influenced by political leaders, and even more often delegates were themselves political leaders, at some level, and consequently able to exercise their own influence in order to become delegates.

The pre-1972 Democratic and Republican conventions were not microcosms of the delegates' states and districts. Delegates were selected by local and state party constituencies that had never heard of affirmative action. They were accountable only in that they expected to return home and lead in the campaign to elect their nominee. Some, of course, were bound by the results of primary elections within their states or by instructions from local or state conventions to vote for a particular candidate, but not many delegates were so bound, and none had been picked and slated by the candidates themselves. For the most part, delegates were not elected in an open process, as is generally the case today, except that the doors by which they entered political and party activity were generally open doors. Obviously corridors beyond the doors were more difficult for women and blacks to navigate, which perhaps was the most damaging flaw in the system. One had to be involved over a period of time to comprehend and participate in the process of being a delegate. That is why the Democrats changed their rules. But still, as Stearns said, most Democrats still cannot comprehend the new rules. Of more crucial significance, the rules today are not working out very well.

The delegates prior to 1972 were not engaged in a giant, selfish conspiracy to seize power. The record shows their selections sometimes were very good, perhaps better than the selections since the rule changes that followed 1968. On the other hand, some delegations in those years were dominated or frustrated by the party leadership or the unit rule, and their independence was bridled. Although it may have been a misapprehension, there was a distinct feeling by many party members that they should seek ways to give the delegates a greater degree of independence from the party leaders. Now our searching question must be, Did the new rules gain more independence for delegates or diminish it?

The 1980 rules, as did the 1972 and 1976 rules—the "new rules"—firmly insisted that a state delegation "shall (1) be broadly representative" and "(2) reflect that State's division of presidential preference."[4] What does "broadly representative" mean? And how do we know for sure what the division of preference is, especially on the day of nomination in a national convention? There are a lot of changes between the selection of Iowa convention delegates in January and the vote in a July convention. A lot of additional things will have been learned about the candidates, or should have been.

The new Democratic rules reject a quota concept. "This goal [full participation by all Democrats, with particular concern for minority groups, native Americans, women, and youth] shall not be accomplished either directly or indirectly by the Party's imposition of mandatory quotas at any level of the delegate selection process."[5] That statement creates a conundrum for a state party because it does not quite mean what it says. Quotas *are* a requirement—indirectly.

Two paragraphs later, the rules say there is nothing wrong with an "equal division . . . of delegate . . . positions between delegate men and delegate women."[6] That statement easily becomes a mandate to provide for such a division, a fifty-fifty quota, but a division that is fair and presents no danger to democracy. Indeed such a split is a distinct political advantage—if the delegates can be selected to be representative rather than appointed just to make the nose count legal.

The major change, the fundamental turnaround dictated by the new rules, requires serious evaluation by the parties as to whether having independent delegates is considered a virtue. The 1980 Democratic rules provide that "State Parties may require presidential candidates to submit demographic information with respect to the delegation allocated to them."[7] A careful look at the evolution of the process will reveal that this provision is the clue to the most significant change in the rules. A reflection of "presidential preference" is *required*. Delegates are picked or approved by the candidates, or more likely, their managers pick the slates, which are "balanced" to avoid criticism from those segments that are left out. The quota system does not have to be explicitly mandated by party rules. It becomes automatic.

That system is not all bad. Quotas invite attention from party leaders and participants to make certain the reach of the party is inclusive. The objection to a quota system is that delegates are picked because of some fact of birth rather than competition for the position on their merits, plus there is hardly any end to claims by other segments of society for their quota assignment. The objection here is not so much to the indirect quota system as to what it indicates—that delegates are picked by candidates, not selected by constituents. The goal of having independent delegates has not been achieved. They are instructed and bound more precisely than when they were bound and driven by the bosses.

The rules grant "to [the] presidential candidate, or that candidate's authorized representative(s)," the veto over any who have filed in support of the candidate. As a practical matter, Democratic candidates pick their own slates, even if under certain circumstances they must approve a minimum of additional names for every delegate position. Rule 6E(1) of the Democratic party's 1980 delegate selection procedures provides that "State Parties may require presidential candidates to submit statements that specify what steps such candidates will take to encourage full participation in their delegate selection process, including, but not limited to, procedures by which persons may file as delegate candidates."[8]

A party member may not just run for a delegate slot—not without being selected or approved by a presidential candidate. This rule has the desired effect of assuring the presence of blacks, youth, women, and others included in quota provisions (or quota concepts), but it has a side effect that perhaps offsets all advantages. It produces delegates of less independence than when they were picked by the bosses, and the parties will have to decide whether the new process is a desirable one. Parties should ponder whether they need a convention at all if a delegate represents a candidate rather than the voting constituency.

Most of the loss of independence in quest of quota representation has been in the Democratic party, and there has been more volatility in its rules. But the Republicans, too, have been affected by a loss of independence for delegates as a result of the present rules that tie the delegates to the candidates.

That change might be unimportant if we could be certain that representing a presidential candidate were roughly the same as representing the constituency. In a presidential primary or caucus it is difficult to determine true voter opinion. The uncertainty has at least three sources. Only a small number of voters participate in the primaries, and an even smaller number participate in the caucus process. Votes are too frequently cast on the basis of superficial media and advertisement impressions, with the voter having little chance to know very much about the candidates. In the case of multiple candidates, only first preferences can be expressed, with no possibility for a consensus expression, and a candidate with a minority of the support often ends up with the most votes.

Circumstances change as the primary voting is carried on over several months, and events and a greater understanding of the candidates' presidential qualifications may change opinions already pledged in concrete. Each candidate cannot be fully examined by each voter, and no candidate can enter with full force the voting process in each state.

On March 20, 1980, the first day of spring, the nominations were closed. It had become (I predicted) an absolute certainty that the voters of the United States would have to choose between Ronald Reagan and Jimmy Carter.[9] It was mathematically impossible for either to have been overtaken. Without debating the qualifications of either, we can be excused for asking (1) Were they truly the best that the parties could offer? (2) Had the voice of democracy really and accurately spoken so swiftly in this manner? (3) Why did we have to go through the ordeal of campaigning, voting, and "deciding" in the thirty-one remaining states? and (4) Did we know what we were doing?

This "lockup" of the process is stark evidence of the change in the process from Franklin D. Roosevelt to Carter and Reagan. "Owning" delegates is different from "having the support" of delegates. There was, on that mid-March day, no longer any realistic opportunity for either party to change its mind.

John Kennedy did not enter the California primary in 1960, leaving all the delegates for Governor Edmund G. (Pat) Brown, the sole entrant, to trade. (There might have been a bargain: Kennedy to be favored if he stayed out of the California primary.) Brown did not trade his delegates; he freed them. They then split about evenly between Kennedy and Stevenson, with a few each to Symington and Johnson and with Brown getting one-half vote. The split was a result of Brown's permitting the delegates to vote as they wished, and probably the delegation's vote reflected what a primary election would have decided among the four if it had been held the day of the convention. California law would have presented all the delegates to one of the candidates, but the significance is that the voters in the primary would not have had the benefit of deliberate decision that was available to the delegates in convention.

The California vote at the 1960 Democratic Convention is an example of what is likely to happen if delegates are not picked on a slate to be bound to the candidate by whom they were slated, are not bound by an election that must take place before the final lines are drawn, and do not vote as a group under unit rule. The California vote is informative as it shows what might happen if we could find a way to elect independent delegates who are free to exercise individual judgment right up to the time of the convention vote, keeping the assorted wishes of the people back home in mind.

The change from delegates controlled or influenced by bosses to delegates owned by candidates was, I contend, a sideward step if not a backward step. It cannot be denied that the motives of the people who wrought the change were good. Even so, questions arise from a comparison of the old procedures and the new rules. Should delegates be picked or slated by anyone or any group other than the voters? Does a primary that does not bind the delegates absolutely to vote in keeping with the expressed position of the voters destroy the usefulness of the primary?

Is it necessary to come up with proportionate numbers of "minority groups, native Americans, women, and youth" in a delegation in order to prove that the delegation is "broadly representative"? Does it make a delegate more, or less, "representative" to be picked by a candidate and placed on a slate to become a delegate only if that candidate wins in the caucus or primary? Whom *should* delegates represent?

It would seem that the John Kennedy nomination combined the best of two worlds, the vitality of the primary elections with the wary judgment of the political workers and party leaders. For whatever reasons, there has not been that same combination since 1960, when the voters guided and advised the convention and the political leaders were wary, perhaps wise, and certainly successful. There was participation, excitement, and credibility. There was consensus. The party and the nation benefited. But, so it was later said, the 1960 delegates were not representative, not under the present rules.

In 1964 Democratic delegates could have been elected or appointed by any method, or drawn by lot from phone books, and Lyndon B. Johnson would have been nominated anyhow. The party leadership, nonetheless, was disturbed by the exclusion of blacks, which was highlighted by a Mississippi Freedom Democratic party delegation that presented itself in opposition to the regular delegation. The seating dispute was resolved, but the issue of a fair and democratic selection of delegates had been raised in a democratic fashion. The time for change had arrived. Blacks had been excluded, or ignored, or given only token delegate positions by most of the states at the Kennedy convention and at all conventions of all parties prior to that one.

In advance of the 1968 Democratic Convention, the Committee on Rules and the Committee on Credentials created a special Commission on the Democratic Selection of Presidential Nominees, headed by the then-governor of Iowa, Harold Hughes.[10] I will dwell on that commission's report because it was made before the McGovern-Fraser reforms and it achieved a clarity not blurred by the Chicago debacle. Noting that events had "called into question the integrity of the convention system for nominating presidential candidates," the commission cited the abuses and traced the history of the convention, concluding, inter alia, that the state systems for selecting delegates and the procedures of the convention

73

"display considerably less fidelity to basic democratic principles than a nation which claims to govern itself can safely tolerate."[11]

Along with some minor matters, the commission made two specific recommendations for immediate adoption, so they would be applicable to the 1968 convention. One, it recommended an end to any racial discrimination, with the burden of proof on the state organizations when discrimination is indicated. Two, it suggested that the convention "abolish the Unit Rule and refuse to enforce instructions by state conventions, state committees, or state primary statutes, that individual delegates be bound to vote in accordance with the preferences of the majority of the delegation."[12] Fair enough! As far as it goes.

The commission observed that "Negroes[13] display a rapidly increasing dissatisfaction with the role of junior partners in the 'Democratic Party'; they are no longer content to permit whites to monopolize the positions of political power."[14] It was during the latter years of the Eisenhower administration, John Kennedy's campaign, and his first years as president that the black citizens, especially the young, began their insistence on full equality. They rode in the front of the bus, they invented sit-ins at lunch counters. They took part in marches and street demonstrations.

The Democratic party, of all American institutions, could not hang back. It had been a difficult generation for black citizens; and it is shameful that the political parties had not been responsive, the Congress had not been responsive, the presidency had not been responsive enough, and finally that only a nondemocratic and nonaccountable institution, the Supreme Court, had breached the walls of segregation. Now in 1968 the Democratic party acknowledged that it must continue to tear away at the walls, and the Republican party was to be not far behind.

There is no justification in the United States for any racial discrimination, no acceptable excuse for any barrier because of color, whether the barrier be to medical school, bank boards, public office, political party activities, or college faculties. Any set of rules designed for the selection of delegates to the national party conventions is not acceptable, and not likely to be accepted, if anyone is put at a disadvantage because of race. Neither should the parties deny that black citizens and members of other previously neglected groups are entitled to some special consideration, some extra official effort.

The 1980 Democratic rules dictate that "discrimination on the basis of race, sex, age, color, national origin, religion, ethnic identity, or economic status [elsewhere there is added 'persons over 65' and 'the physically handicapped'] in the conduct of Democratic Party affairs is prohibited."[15] The 1980 Republican rules declare that the Republicans are to "provide for full participation with equal opportunity for men and women, for minorities and heritage groups, and for all Americans regardless of age or social or economic status."[16]

These declarations are not automatic, of course. As the Hughes Commission urged, "it is up to the Convention itself and the Credentials Committee to see that mandate is not twisted into an excuse for mere tokenism."[17] The Democratic rules seem to assure that there will be an appropriate number of blacks in each delegation. The Republican party seems just as dedicated, if less specific.

The changes parties must make in the nominating process must not diminish the ever-widening role of the minority citizen in the process. The changes suggested in this book would enhance that role, as well as add a recognition of maturity in race relations, of the achievements of black citizens in politics, and of dignity of the individual participant.

Notes

1. John F. Kennedy, Inaugural Address, in Theodore C. Sorensen, *Kennedy* (New York: Harper & Row, 1965), pp. 245 and 248.

2. James W. Davis, *Presidential Primaries: Road to the White House* (New York: Thomas Y. Crowell Company, 1967), pp. 1–2.

3. "Is There a Better Method of Picking Presidential Nominees?" *New York Times*, 2 December 1979, sec. 4, p. E5.

4. *Delegate Selection Rules for the 1980 Democratic National Convention* by John C. White, Chairman (Washington, D.C.: Democratic National Committee, 1978), p. 3.

5. Ibid., p. 7.

6. Ibid.

7. Ibid., p. 8.

8. Ibid.

9. "President and Reagan Now Appear Likely Contenders in Fall Elections," *New York Times*, 20 March 1980, p. A1; and "Political Machinery and Windmills," *New York Times*, 20 March 1980, p. A26.

10. U.S., Congress, House, *Report of Commission on the Democratic Selection of Presidential Nominees*, 90th Cong., 2d sess., 14 October 1968, *Congressional Record*, 114:31544–31560.

11. Ibid., p. 31545.

12. Ibid.

13. This was the acceptable word in 1968.

14. *Congressional Record*, 114:31546.

15. *Delegate Selection Rules for the 1980 Democratic National Convention*, p. 6.

16. *Rules Adopted by the 1976 Republican National Convention* (Kansas City, Mo.: Lowell Press, 1976), p. 3.

17. *Congressional Record*, 114:31545.

8

Bosses Versus Primaries

Estes Kefauver contributed as much to the efficacy of the presidential primaries as anybody, and he pointed the way for John Kennedy, Eugene McCarthy, George McGovern, and Jimmy Carter. Kefauver additionally furnished Ronald Reagan and Edward Kennedy with proof, as Eugene McCarthy was to do, that a sitting president could be challenged through the primaries. The night of July 25, 1952, when Kefauver strode to the podium with Senator Paul Douglas to release Kefauver's delegates, may also mark the beginning of the modern reforms to open up the presidential selection process in the United States, to make the process more democratic.

Kefauver was not the first to use the primaries effectively. Champ Clark received an even sharper slap than Kefauver endured forty years later, but there were only twelve primaries in 1912, there was no television, and there was the two-thirds rule. The Republicans in 1912 also gave an example of a convention's disregard of the results of the primaries. Theodore Roosevelt beat William Howard Taft in ten out of eleven primary elections, but Taft won 566 to 107 on the first ballot. There were serious repercussions, including the Bull Moose party and the election of Woodrow Wilson, but the time for reform had not come.

Primaries were of little significance in either party in 1920, although Republicans cast over 3 million votes in twenty states. Warren Harding was on the ballot in three—he finished a poor fourth in Indiana and Montana and had less than a majority in his native Ohio. In 1928 Herbert Hoover and Alfred E. Smith led comfortably but not remarkably in their respective parties, but other factors assured their nominations. A U.S. senator, Joseph France of Maryland, received more votes and entered more primaries than did President Hoover in 1932, but nonetheless Hoover was given the honor of going against Franklin Roosevelt. Primaries simply were not important.[1]

In 1944 Harold Stassen saw the value of what Kefauver was to learn, or reveal, eight years later. Stassen believed the Republican primaries would be his most available gate to the presidential race, but he was merely testing his speed that year. He was in the process of getting better known. He had served as a young and nationally visible governor of Minnesota, had a prominent position in the navy during World War II, and was a part of the U.S. delegation in the creation of the United Nations. It was in 1948 that Stassen jolted the Republican establishment by excellent showings in four primaries. But Thomas Dewey did well, too, and Stassen's people couldn't cry "stolen" as Clark and Kefauver partisans did.

Stassen changed the campaign style for the Republicans. Kefauver's 1952 experience changed campaigning in the Democratic party and was the omen of reform in delegate selection. Stevenson had to campaign assiduously in the 1956 primaries, and although he won or held his own, Kefauver had mandated the new rules for seeking the nomination.

The Republicans did not have much need for primaries in 1952 because of the availability of General Eisenhower, although his backers did enter him in most of the primaries to illustrate his vote-getting appeal. Robert Taft had the edge with the "regulars," but he had never done well in the primaries. Had Taft not reached the peak of his recognition and accomplishments during the time when war heroes were returning, in all likelihood he would have been nominated and quite possibly elected—if he could have won without going through the process of campaigning in primaries and using television. That the emerging process puts an able but unglamorous person like Taft at a distinct disadvantage is a flaw in the nominating process that cannot be summarily dismissed.

Richard Nixon used the primaries to his advantage, Ronald Reagan used them like magic, and Barry Goldwater was saved by the California primary. The pattern has changed. No longer may a candidate ignore the primaries, nor should we have a system that would permit success without a testing of the voters' opinions.

There are, obviously, disadvantages and dangers to a society that relies indiscriminately on the popular vote. The United States cannot be run like a town meeting. And the United States is not going to be run by a council of elders. Still, both of those approaches have something to be said for them. Kennedy used the town meeting to prove to the elders that he should be the chief.

Let's look more closely at the Democratic Convention of 1952. Five-term Congressman Estes Kefauver had come quickly from unknown to celebrated and had overwhelmed the E. H. "Boss" Crump machine by taking a seat in the Senate in 1948. He had acquired a coonskin cap as his political trademark and had quickly gained national notoriety and acclaim as chairman of the Senate Crime Investigating Committee, set up by legislation written by him to fight organized crime. He had also established a reputation as a dogged individual in the Senate, going his independent way as he saw it.

Harry Truman was president and had been for almost seven years, but he was eligible to run again and had given no clear indication of his plans. The lanky freshman senator from Tennessee decided that he would run, so he called on the president and told him so. President Truman's political instinct to not show his hand let Kefauver go away thinking that Truman didn't mind, but it was an affront to President Truman to be forced to make a decision before he was ready. It also was an embarrassment to be drawn into the New Hampshire presidential primary, and it was an even greater irritation when Kefauver, who had crisscrossed the state shaking hands and did not mind being compared to Abraham Lincoln, received all the delegates by leading the voting 20,000 to 16,000.

President Truman announced that he would not run again. Probably he had always intended to step down, but it can now be argued in retrospect that Kefauver's impatience set the political bosses against him and cost him the nomination. The events also pointed up the need for reform. Yet, in an ironic fashion, the 1952 nominating process brought to the forefront of American life one of its most remarkable public servants, Adlai E. Stevenson. Except for President Truman and the other political leaders, bosses if you will, Stevenson would have remained a relatively obscure former governor of Illinois, and Estes Kefauver would have been the nominee granted the dubious distinction of running against Dwight D. Eisenhower.

Could Kefauver have defeated Eisenhower? Probably no Democratic candidate could have, but Estes Kefauver struck a long-untouched nerve in the American voter, and he just might have overcome the wartime glamour of Eisenhower. Would Kefauver have made a good to outstanding president? Probably. But Stevenson would have also—maybe a remarkable and historic one. The convention did not make a mistaken choice. Many people argued that ignoring the stated preference of the voters was the mistake. Many others argued that Kefauver's wins were in uncontested primaries for the most part and that there was no stated preference. Harry

Truman said primaries were "eyewash." Certainly Kefauver had not been tested against Stevenson.

Adlai E. Stevenson was not an aggressive or a personally ambitious man. Kefauver was, but that fact does not denigrate him, for those are worthy traits. Stevenson, although surely flattered and gratified at the prospect of the presidency, probably would never have set out to seek it on his own. He was sought out for the job, albeit by the so-called bosses.

Here we have two outstanding men, both of whom had the qualities of character, intellect, and ability demanded by the presidency. One chose to charge down one path, and the second wandered rather inadvertently down the other.

The question is, can we afford a system that eliminates either kind of person? Can we afford to disregard the expressed responses of the voters, and can we exclude from the presidency those philosophically disinclined to press strongly their own political fortunes? Both methods of selection are commendable. Neither is uniquely better than the other, although I would prefer that we seek the candidate.

Kefauver in 1952 entered all of the fourteen primaries except the one in Minnesota,[2] but he did not necessarily win enough, and he had no patent on the nomination as he arrived at the Chicago convention. He had lost to Richard Russell in Florida, but except for California and New Hampshire, that was the only place he faced determined opposition. Minnesota went to Hubert H. Humphrey, although write-ins gave Kefauver one-fourth as many votes as Humphrey. Kefauver had won in twelve states with a total of 406 convention votes. He never got more than 362 votes in the convention, but he got those from thirty-three states. The Illinois, Massachusetts, New Jersey, and Pennsylvania primaries were won by Kefauver; the convention votes of those states went mostly to Stevenson, but those delegates were not selected by the primary voters.

Nothing much is certain in politics—past, present, or projective—but it can be argued convincingly that had the

81

1972 Democratic rules been applicable in 1952, Estes Kefauver would have captured the nomination and Adlai Stevenson might not have been even a footnote in presidential campaign history.

James W. Davis wrote that "one of the last of the old Progressive measures to be enacted, the presidential primary system remains as controversial today as it was when it was introduced by reform-minded legislators early in the twentieth century." Davis assembled a sample of pre-1972 arguments for and against presidential primaries.

"1. It permits rank-and-file voters in a limited number of states to participate directly in the selection of presidential candidates while leaving the ultimate decision to the delegates of the highest representative party council, the national nominating convention." Were this state of affairs still true, which it is not, it would be difficult to find fault with the broad concept of presidential primaries.

"2. It creates a healthy voter interest and general public concern with the nominating process—more so than does the state party convention system." This argument is certainly true.

"3. It serves as a testing ground for presidential candidates, and it gives the national convention delegates and the voting public the opportunity to assess at firsthand a presidential candidate's behavior, reaction under pressure, and statesman-like qualities."[3] This factor is an excellent justification for primaries.

James W. Davis's arguments *against* the presidential primary are several, but six seem relevant for our purposes. All can be overcome or discounted.

1. The span of time from first to last primary is too long.

2. There is "too much psychological importance" attached to the results.

3. "Defeat in a single primary may cut down a leading contender and eliminate him from the race."

4. Votes are more likely to be based on campaigning ability than on competence.

5. "Some qualified presidential aspirants who are important federal or state officeholders" cannot take time to campaign in so many primaries.

6. "The most serious objection to the presidential primary system is that it weakens party responsibility. While the primaries may have weakened intraparty democracy . . . the primaries have had a salutary effect upon the nominating process. . . . This change has occurred without forcing party leadership to relinquish ultimate control over the final selection of the party nominations at the national convention. But it has caused party leaders to think twice before voting against a presidential candidate who has won several hotly contested primaries."[4] No longer do delegates have the luxury of thinking twice. Now they do not need to think at all.

These pro and con arguments were made years before the 1972 rule changes. Those changes, by eliminating the deliberative body of delegates and bringing on, inadvertently, a doubling of the number of primaries, influence all these arguments— making the "con" more persuasive and the "pro" less accurate.

Because of his personality and failures, Kefauver started the move to more reliance on primary elections. Has this been a good move? Do the Democrats have an improved chance today to pick a better presidential candidate than they did in 1952 when they chose Adlai Stevenson over Estes Kefauver, Averell Harriman, and Richard Russell?

Were the conventions that nominated McGovern and Carter all that superior to the conventions that nominated Humphrey and Stevenson? I don't think any of them were as good as the political parties are capable of designing.

Notes

1. James W. Davis, *Presidential Primaries: Road to the White House* (New York: Thomas Y. Crowell Company, 1967), pp. 72 and 73.

2. Ibid., p. 299.

3. Ibid., pp. 252–253.

4. Ibid., pp. 254–260.

9

Distorted Voice

The danger of democracy is that democracy's voice, at least in the presidential search, has been channeled and structured, distorted by artificial time schedules, and limited by rules that pretend to extend democracy. Democracy's voice, as it were, is amplified through a false or flawed system. When William Jennings Bryan spoke to the crowds at great field rallies, his booming voice reached the uttermost ends of the wheat rows. In the convention halls he could be heard when others could not. Most statesmen and would-be statesmen of the day could not equal that volume. As it turned out, the candidate with the loudest voice received the nomination three times, but he was not elected to the presidency.

Public address systems, invented and gradually improved, spread the voice of the candidates, and telecommunication soon extended the voice and ultimately the view, finally in living color (or what purports to be), to all the precincts. All the while, political parties were feeling the tug and push to do the same for democracy's voice. The history of political parties marks the regular effort, often in spurts and sometimes tentatively, to permit a widening number of people to participate in the political process. Generally, the communications technicians have been more successful than the technicians of political structures. As Albert Einstein said long ago, politics is harder than physics.

When John F. Kennedy spoke in October of 1961 at Kenan Field, the University of North Carolina's football stadium, technicians, observing wisely among themselves that the requirements for football announcing and for a presidential address from the end zone were likely to be different, spent several days adjusting the system and redirecting the horns that sit atop the tall poles. On the morning of the speech the security people noted that the horns had been pointed in what seemed to them the wrong direction. So, being Secret Service men, they suspected sabotage and hurriedly had the loudspeakers moved back to the positions they had been in. One dear old lady sitting in the stands, brought up in the discipline and pretenses of the academic world, turned to her companion after the president had spoken for a few moments and whispered in profound and excited amazement, "Isn't he brilliant? He's speaking in Latin!"

In presidential nominations the voice of democracy speaks, if it is democracy's voice at all, in distorted tones and often with misdirected aim, but that doesn't mean that the parties tinkering with the public address system have not acted in good faith. Too often, however, they get Latin instead of English.

Consider the primaries. Heralded as the ultimate in permitting the full and mighty voice of the people to overwhelm the whispered conspiracies of the party bosses, legislature after legislature has voted to extend democracy's public address system with various voting arrangements. It is not the variety that is bad. That, in the spirit of our intended federalism, has been the best feature about the new arrangements. They have provided the multiple experiments that permit us to sort out and select far wiser arrangements.

However, as we have seen, primaries have increasingly attracted the "one-issue" voter. They have frequently brought out the "emotional vote" on an issue not necessarily presidential and exploited by a candidate more demagogic than presidential. Often primaries have mobilized a total vote that is of a disgracefully low percentage. Sometimes in the early stages of a campaign season they have locked in delegate positions that have become irrelevant or outdated by the end of the season; or if held at the end of the season, some primaries have permitted a victory surge or a death blow that hardly was desired—not in that place or circumstance—by the party voters. Both early and late primaries have exercised, first in the minds of the press and then seeping back through the media distillery to the minds of democracy, an inordinate and occasionally unfair influence.

As David Broder has observed, "The power of selection has been given to the people—but under circumstances and conditions that are almost guaranteed to distort the public choice."[1]

The strongest argument for a new philosophy in presidential nominations is that we *must* change.

> Otherwise we may be beginning a slow, confused descent into an era of what Walter Dean Burham has called "politics without parties." Political adventurers will roam the countryside like Chinese warlords or Iranian ayatollahs, recruiting personal armies, conducting hostilities against some rival warlords and forming alliances with others, and, as they win elections, striving to govern through ad hoc coalitions in legislatures.[2]

Kay Lawson has raised another interesting doubt about the true voice of democracy.

> The self-nominated candidate, operating through a personal network varying greatly in magnitude and efficiency, but only slightly in style, from the old *café cabals* supporting the independent candidates of pre-nineteenth century politics, may well have made his return. . . .
>
> If the presidential primary comes to be a major means of pre-

convention vote gathering will that institution—and the opportunity it offers the average member to participate in his party's
nominating process—be strengthened? Will this give the rank-and-
file membership a meaningful say in party nominations or merely
subject him to a longer season of campaign oratory?[3]

Primaries have added hoopla and tremendous costs to the
presidential search, which is not all bad. We see our leaders in
action, but who wants to remember America's candidates for
the "most powerful elected post in the world" either huddling
in a donkey cart being pulled through a snowy New Hampshire
street or riding a bicycle, perhaps even backward, through the
sands of a Florida beach?

The presidential primaries put a demanding physical
strain, as well as a financial one, on the candidates. Perhaps
trial by physical ordeal is not all bad. Heaven knows physical
stamina is necessary in the White House. The foot soldier in
the Ardennes Forest could remember the ordeal of training
maneuvers and comfort himself by saying to his buddy
dodging German eighty-eights, "Well this ain't as bad as
Tennessee." But is that the way to be tested for the presidency?

The sound technicians can boost the actual voice of a
speaker, they can step the system up to clarify and extend
the voice impulses. Thus, to move to the political analogy, we
look for an amplification of democracy in our search for a
president, but we find that the voice in the convention is not
at all an amplification of the democratic voice from back
home. The booster process of delegate selection has distorted
the voice.

It was argued that the political bosses spoke for themselves
and their own continuing influences, not with the voice of
the democracy. Under the present rules the delegates to the
American presidential convention usually do not have constituencies. Therefore, it can be argued that since they represent no constituency or only pretend to do so, they cannot
amplify or boost the voice of democracy because they do

not speak for the people from whom they came.

The bosses had constituencies, and although the bosses frequently cut their constituents off and spoke only for themselves and their own personal interests, the bosses nevertheless pledged allegiance to a constituency. Not so today's delegates. They represent, somehow, not the constituency whence they come; they represent, curiously, a candidate. The loudspeakers are pointed in the wrong direction.

The situation is exactly backward. If people are assembled as delegates in a convention to make a choice on behalf of their fellow party members, why are they not representing their constituents? Why, otherwise, should we have a convention? How, indeed, did that situation come about? The political leaders wanted to be fair, to bring more people into participation, and to make democracy's voice strong and clear in the selection of the presidency, removing that process from what was imagined to be, sometimes accurately, the clutches of the special interests. The political leaders failed.

The reforms of the parties had the effect of diminishing the influence of the parties, maybe leading to their destruction. Doubtless some people who took part in bringing about the reforms intended such a result and would fight all efforts to retard the antiparty influences. The important instrument to be preserved is not political parties as such but a sensible method of choosing our president. Many who would destroy party organization have the image of the old city political machine that was disdainful of the democratic process. That this is not generally the shape of state and local party organizations today is not the most relevant concern either. The question remains, How best can the people of the United States elect the best possible person as their president?

Would it matter if national political parties were wiped out? "The Republic would not collapse, at least not right away," observed Austin Ranney. Rather, "the candidate organizations, the women's caucuses, the black caucuses, the right-to-life leagues, and the like would become the only real players in the game."[4] Add to those groups the U.S. Chamber of Commerce, the labor unions, the Association of Manufacturers, the bankers, and every other group that does not want to feel left out of the national politics. If we should move to a national primary, "the mass communication media," suggested Ranney, "would become the sole agencies for sorting out the finalists from the original entrants and for defining the voters' choices." And if the parties are wiped out, "the societal functions of interest-aggregation, consensus-building, and civil war–prevention would presumably be left to the schools, the churches, and perhaps Common Cause and Nader's Raiders."[5] The republic might not collapse, but it would be severely endangered.

For two centuries the American political parties have afforded a consensus-building apparatus, and parties came into being in the United States because of the need for consensus in a diverse and democratic land. How did it happen that the parties have sown the seeds of their own destruction? With the best of intentions they were pursuing the most worthy of objectives. They wanted to increase the citizens' power and opportunity to shape the destiny of the nation by increasing the citizens' voice in the selection of the president. Even the bosses wanted to increase the credibility, and therefore the effectiveness, of the party.

Reformers in the social sciences, including political institutions and welfare programs, are loath to admit that an experiment they engineered is not working out so well. Chemists or physicists, in their labs, readily admit that an experiment didn't work, throw it out and start over, or refine it and proceed, so it should not be such a difficult ordeal for party national committee members to wonder out loud whether their rules are working as they intended.

We should not want to see the two-party system fade away because it is difficult to envision any institution of a democratic society that could take over its consensus-building mission. Without such an institution, we would be in quadrennial danger of nominating, and therefore electing, a president by chance and not by plan. As a matter of stark reality, we are already in such danger.

The new party rules, or some of them, threaten the stability and even the survival of the political party structure. It does not serve us well to require that a presidential candidate must approve those delegates who would stand pledged to that candidate. It does not serve us well that in practice the candidate generally picks his own slate. In the quest for conventions that are more representative, we find ourselves with conventions not of delegates committed to representing their own people but of delegates committed emotionally, legally, and sometimes obdurately to a particular candidate. The reforms were intended to assure a candidate the support of a number of delegates in keeping with the number of votes the candidate received in the caucus or primary. The price for that worthy objective has been too expensive.

There are three results that indicate the new delegate selection rule has not worked out as well as originally imagined. It creates a candidate-oriented convention, which is acceptable, if not desirable, for the purpose of nominating a candidate. The convention, however, is the supreme governing authority of the party with responsibility for policy and the setting and resetting of rules and procedures. Delegates elected as the representative of a candidate, instead of a constituency within the party, are naturally primarily concerned with the nomination of their candidate and at best have only a secondary or a short-term interest in maintaining and running the party.

The party governance may survive in a convention of candidate-oriented delegates, but it is not the ideal climate. In fact, such a convention almost assures a little erosion of party strength at each convention until in due time there is no party and no continuing structure for politics.

Structure and stability sometimes obstruct needed progress, but more often they serve us well by helping us maintain our bearings as we attempt to progress. We do not fare so well without some order in our affairs. It would not be accurate to describe our national presidential nominating process as Iranian-like participatory politics, but a visitor from Mars would have some trouble in discerning the difference since it is not likely that the visitor would speak either Persian or English.

Another doubt raised by this rule of candidate selection of delegates relates to the integrity of the convention itself. Does it add to the convention's credibility to know that the delegates did not come as independent and thoughtful party representatives engaged in one of the more awesome tasks of American politics, choosing a possible president? Does this method of selecting delegates add to the public's confidence in the political system? To be sure, it seems to be preferable to having a convention dominated by bosses, but is a convention dominated by candidates or a single candidate (given the deadly primary peel-off derby) all that superior? Is it not possible that the candidates who dominate a convention might take an even narrower view of the public good than did the working local and state party leaders (bosses, if you will) who dominated conventions in the past?

Women and minority members were left out of the "bosses conventions," but are they really an influential part of the "candidates conventions"? There are more of them, true, but do they exercise much independent judgment? As delegates are they in a position of influence, or is their presence merely a sop, a token presence, a possible insult, even a fraud? That is, are they there because their judgment is respected, as it should be? Or is their presence merely to give the *appearance* of representation? Would it not be better if we had a system that would draw in women and minority delegates because each had an intellectual and political contribution to make rather than because the party wants superficial "proof" that it is broad and fair? Is it not preferable to have a system that elects, rather than "slates," women and minority members?

The candidates convention is not likely to be equal, let alone superior, to the bosses convention if we are primarily concerned about the future of conventions, presidential leadership, and steady, if not stable, political structures as well as a long and sure future for the nation. The delegate-selected-by-a-candidate rule, it seems, has taken a bad turn.

In his 1952 acceptance speech, Adlai Stevenson declared, "Even more important than winning the election is governing the Nation. That is the test of a political party—the acid, final test."[6] Austin Ranney, in an interview, touched the heart of the predicament.

> Many people have been thinking some about this whole new Presidential selection system, actually in creation since 1968, and I find that often that question is answered from one or the other of two points of view: (1) The virtue-is-its-own-reward school whose proponents say the system is a lot more open now than it used to be, a lot more fair, more democratic, more decent. (2) The by-their-fruits-ye-shall-know-them school which asks: Better than what? Has it produced a better quality of candidates or strengthened the parties or increased popular confidence in the political process? I am of this latter persuasion.[7]

Those of us who have worked in the past for adequate participation by women and members of minority groups cannot contend that the objective of participation is more important than the objective of the nominating process. How do we achieve a workable process and at the same time preserve those gains in demographic representation? The parties must design and promote better affirmative action plans; if we try to achieve balanced representation by artificial inventions, we clog up the machinery.

Notes

1. David S. Broder, "Primaries Full of Paradox," *The News and Observer,* Raleigh, North Carolina, 9 June 1976, p. 5.

2. Arthur M. Schlesinger, Jr., "Crisis of the Party System: II," *Wall Street Journal,* 14 May 1979, p. 20.

3. Kay Lawson, *Political Parties and Democracy in the United States* (New York: Charles Scribner's Sons, 1968), p. 142.

4. Austin Ranney, "The Political Parties: Reform and Decline," in *The New American Political System,* ed. Anthony King (Washington, D.C.: American Enterprise Institute for Public Policy Research, 1979), p. 247.

5. Ibid.

6. "Acceptance Speech by Governor Adlai E. Stevenson," July 26, 1952, in *History of American Presidential Elections,* vol. 4, *1940-1968,* ed. Arthur M. Schlesinger, Jr. (New York: Chelsea House Publishers, 1971), p. 3295.

7. "Is There a Better Method of Picking Presidential Nominees?" *New York Times,* 2 December 1979, sec. 4, p. E5.

10

Danger of Democracy

The latent danger to any society is that change will be resisted, dissent will be repressed or ignored, and voices then will become violence. By some vision and some luck, not by wisdom written into the Constitution but by fortuitous moves based on our British heritage and the freedom philosophy of the Constitution, a political party system was established in the United States that has accommodated dissent and change, but by no means perfectly. Passing over "what might have been" in the years of Abraham Lincoln and Stephen A. Douglas, the people of the United States had great difficulty in listening to the dissatisfactions of the industrial worker, the black citizen, and aspiring women and had to be variously dragged, although not yet all the way, into changes that mean that workers and blacks are treated as human beings and women are treated as the equals of men. The political party system accommodated, although not without ordeal and strife, the thickening opposition to a pointless war. The accommodations, however, were not accomplished without resistance from established institutions, including political parties.

The sturdiness of our society's structure, compared not to an ideal but to the rest of the world, is borne out by the changes political parties did bring about, reluctantly or not, in response to "outside" voices. Political parties were, and still are, the open forum for all kinds of causes and a multitude of groups.

One or the other of the two major political parties generally serves as the "outside" voice to government. It was this aspect of political parties that George Washington disliked, but it can be argued that this aspect has more than once preserved the republic. Political parties became the political cutting edge for the rights of labor, minorities, and women, substantially giving expression to those causes before they were taken up by the government. Women regularly urged voting rights to the party conventions long before passage of the Nineteenth Amendment. An essential function of political parties is to communicate between the people and their government. The side effects of reforms that alter national party structure, function, and vitality may outweigh the value of the actual reforms. Political parties must remain sensitive to their public duty to keep open the lines of communication.

Such a public duty means the political party must keep its doors open, be well advertised, and even go out into the street to recruit, cajole, and lead new members to its fireside. The new rules promote this party posture. Political parties must be suitably designed for channeling aspirations and responding to dissent, to be available for the expression of ideas, even unlikely ones, and sensitive to criticism. The political party must not only be there, it must make its members feel at home and feel it is the place where they can say what needs to be said.

To be sure, political parties are not the exclusive channel for the expression of ideas, and it is equally true that the party cannot be the voice of every dissatisfaction or the champion of every cause. A multitude of lobbyists and national headquarters, by whatever name, clutter Washington, and that is as it should be. Individuals and dissident groups picket city halls, nuclear plants, and foreign embassies and demonstrate in the streets and wherever else they choose. The political party's unique contribution is its capacity to develop consensus, to draw together groups and interests, to seek the common ground, and to give the minority the majority's support when appropriate. The political party gives structure to dissent and opposition as well as to creative progress.

The integrity of this mission must be protected by a stance of openness. That we have two major parties reinforces that integrity. That we have political parties makes the government representative, and those people who respond with a shrug of the shoulder to warnings that parties are being weakened to the point of death simply have not thought of the alternatives.

Most political scientists, perhaps all, will agree that "The wisdom of having political parties long ago ceased to be debatable; they are essential to the governance of free societies."[1] To put it another way,

> The basic change that is needed, though, is simply a renewed appreciation of what useful things parties—as institutions and not just as labels—are to have around. If this should somehow come to pass, it would then be relatively easy to rebuild the parties as instruments for planning and representation within what must be recognized as a now-irreversible feature of the U.S. nominee-selection process—the widespread use of direct primaries. Restoring the organized parties to vigorous health and giving them back their central role in the presidential-selection process should be the No. 1 reform objective of the next decade.[2]

The political parties can now set before all but the lethargic the chance to participate in the formulation of national policy and the selection of the national leader. Whatever the party does elsewhere in states or cities, it cannot evade

97

society's charge to make participation in national direction available to all citizens. Thus the political party, by accommodating variety and by listening and translating, ensures the stability of representative democracy. It also helps assure the vitality and progress of democratic government.

One danger is that an unstructured and a careless selection of presidents and the resultant impatience with the solving of problems will lead the people to elect a "tough and strong" president, again in a careless manner, and then to provide him with a white horse when he calls for one—as Italy embraced Mussolini. It is ineffective self-government that seeks and accepts the strong man who becomes a dictator. Such an occurrence is less likely, some would say impossible, in the United States. We have many safeguards and safety valves, structured balances and cross-checks, and a predilection for freedom. Yet we exist in an uncertain world, and one of the best hopes for the world and for free people is the continued effectiveness of the self-government of the United States. The place of the political party in maintaining that effectiveness should not be discounted. Political parties, opposed to one another, must be open and alive, and they must be nurtured and preserved, even cherished.

Essentially the reforms of the Democratic party that have taken place since 1964, and to a lesser but a significant extent of the Republican party, have had as their thrust an opening up to accommodate more and more people and their views. These efforts have strengthened the political parties, it can be argued, although many wonder how, and others read into the changes the weakening and demise of political parties.

The collective actions of the two major political parties have demonstrated that they understand their mission and obligations, and they have moved to accommodate a revolutionary insistence that the people of the United States are no longer willing to be left out of the conduct of their affairs. That inherent danger has been overcome and is being overcome.

The counterdanger has always been that the rush to reform will bring, instead of new strength, a Babylonian disorder, so that in the end we will be unable to synthesize and communicate clear directions for the future and will be capable of choosing effective leadership only by the grace of God. In time, so much uncertain leadership, confused national directions, political disorder, and instability can also lead, if not to the "strong man," to our acceptance of inadequate and untried leadership. It is possible for an excess of democracy, that is to say, a lack of structured political parties, to lead to the destruction of representative government or, as is more likely in our time, to its gradual disintegration.

It is inevitable that a sloppy and disorganized method of nominating presidential candidates is an imminent danger. If our process makes it impossible to know what we are getting until we have got it, if our process does not ensure that we attract the best possible men and women to the presidential candidacy, we may very well elect an inadequate president, or a succession of inadequate presidents, until we come to the point of desperation that renders us willing to change drastically our definition of democracy. The grace of God may not dwell with us forever. It is far better that we give some attention to shaping up the way we use our political parties to choose our presidents.

Milton S. Eisenhower, university president, served in some capacity every president from Calvin Coolidge to Richard Nixon, and his account of this service, along with his other far-reaching activities, is full of sage advice. He devoted a chapter to national party conventions, noting that radical changes are imperative. He wrote that

> a society which insists on running its quadrennial conventions like circuses should not be surprised to get tightrope walkers as presidential candidates.
>
> The selection of presidential and vice-presidential candidates should be a profound exercise of representative government—an

exercise that would command the pride and enthusiastic support of the American people. As it is, this important task is carried out under conditions that are comparable to those of a carnival, circus, or prize fight.

If each of the two major political parties is to nominate the individual best prepared to meet the awesome responsibilities of the President of the United States, we must take prompt steps to reform substantially the national conventions. I am convinced that changes must be made in the selection of delegates and in the rules of the conventions themselves, especially the rules and traditions involving the nomination of the presidential and vice-presidential candidates.[3]

The danger of democracy is that we will use its name in vain, and in its name so unstructure our political institutions that nothing can be decided, or decided wisely. There is considerable evidence that we have come close to doing just that to our political parties.

It is not that too much democracy is a mean goal. It may not be possible to get too much, although it is conceivable that we can get too much of a good thing, as I discovered about strawberry shortcake at the age of eight. We must not forget that the democratic voice, in a large society, is often best expressed through representative government and that participatory democracy, if not a redundancy, is generally most wisely expressed by full, equal, and fair participation in the selection of democracy's representatives who then, as accountable representatives, treat the complex issues.

The danger of democracy is not that democracy is dangerous, but that we somehow bring ourselves to believe that the democracy of the town hall can be extended to nationwide decisions. The danger of democracy thus becomes a danger that we will lose democracy in our attempt to gain more of it. We do not expect to decide a national energy policy by referendum, voting on eight or ten proposals put forward by eight or ten groups. That issue is too complex even for 535 members of Congress. We expect the national administration—the president, that is—to present a program to be picked over and refined or altered by the Congress, and we are ready, if the members of Congress displease us enough in the way they pick, to deal with them individually at the next election.

Yet we expect to pick our president, a far more complex determination and infinitely more important than even an energy policy, by participatory disorder that knows no equal in American society.

> Specialists now conduct campaigns. The men who understand the Media Map are the media masters. In the back rooms they are joined by other specialists—in public-opinion polling, in direct mail, in street and telephone canvassing, in ethnic analysis. Anyone who has the direct ear of the candidate is now styled a "strategist"; the old-fashioned hatchet man out on the road is now styled a "surrogate." And the road itself has changed. Secret Service men protect the candidate's body and armed police patrol rallies from rooftops, scouting for assassins.[4]

Where is the clear understanding and deliberative thought by the voter?

There is a unique book written by James David Barber of Duke University about presidential character and the way to predict it.[5] Voters make a prediction, at least to themselves, when each casts a vote for president. They have impressions from what they see, hear, and read based on what they want or think they want. This body of information is gathered by other people and is presented by other people, some of whom are truthful and some of whom are manipulative.

Barber, among other things, provided a yardstick for measuring what one learns about a candidate, a way to judge what kind of president the candidate likely will become. This yardstick is an invaluable tool for the voter. An exercise in measuring will help the voters even if they arrive at a variety of conclusions or, having reached similar conclusions, vote differently because they seek different objectives for the nation. It is an improvement in voter self-education to think about "the five concepts—character, world view, style, power situation, and climate of expectations." It is helpful for the voter to have a grid on which to place his or her information and impressions.

"The President," wrote Barber, "is a man with a memory in a system with a history. Like all of us, he draws on his past to shape his future. The pathetic hope that the White House will turn a Caligula into a Marcus Aurelius is as naive as the fear that ultimate power inevitably corrupts. The problem is to understand—and to state understandably—what in the personal past foreshadows the Presidential future."[6] The problem is to understand—but the greater problem is to have the facts.

Joe McGinniss firmly established in the American language the phrase, "the selling of the president."[7] He was describing the 1968 presidential campaign of Richard M. Nixon, but his work applies, unfortunately, to far more presidential candidates than Nixon. "Politics," McGinniss observed, "in a sense, has always been a con game." The same is true of advertising, he said, so "it is not surprising then, that politicians and advertising men should have discovered one another. And, once they recognized that the citizen did not so much vote for a candidate as make a psychological purchase of him, not surprising that they began to work together."[8]

Television is particularly adaptable to the selling of a president. According to McGinniss,

> With the coming of television, and the knowledge of how it could be used to seduce voters, the old political values disappeared. Something new, murky, undefined started to rise from the mists. "In all countries," Marshall McLuhan writes, "the party system has folded like the organization chart. Policies and issues are useless for election purposes, since they are too specialized and hot. The shaping of a candidate's integral image has taken the place of discussing conflicting points of view."[9]

Barber gave the right guidelines for an intelligent analysis of presidential candidates, but you cannot measure what you do not have. You can't hit the ball if you can't see it.

Barber's message is, "look to character first." But how? "Character is the force, the motive power, around which the person gathers his view of the world and from which his style receives its impetus. The issues will change, the character of the President will last."[10] But how does the voter in New Hampshire or Florida or Illinois know what history, what accomplishments, what examples of integrity, what spark of creativity, what resoluteness, what compassion, or what dedication there are in the would-be president to be able to measure it by any standard?

There would be a revolutionary departure in presidential politics if every voter could read James David Barber's book and others that help the reader assess qualifications; it is extremely beneficial that these books are available to commentators and columnists. Still, having read the book, the voters need to know the facts. They are not going to get them from television spots, from handshaking tours, from superficial interviews, or from "campaign literature."

Even if the first several months of campaigning miraculously reveal the traits the voter must judge, it probably will be too late to do any judging. The ones who might have measured better are out of it. That is our system.

We need to find a way to use the measuring sticks based on observation of past presidents in action. We need to find a way to gather and understand the information to be measured. That is not our system.

Notes

1. Stephen Hess, *The Presidential Campaign: The Leadership Selection Process After Watergate* (Washington, D.C.: Brookings Institution, 1974), p. 101.

2. Everett Carll Ladd, Jr., " 'Reform' Is Wrecking the U.S. Party System," *Fortune*, November 1977, p. 188.

3. Milton S. Eisenhower, *The President Is Calling* (Garden City, N.Y.: Doubleday & Company, 1974), p. 395.

4. Theodore H. White, "The Making of the President Ain't What It Used to Be," *Life*, February 1980, p. 67.

5. James David Barber, *The Presidential Character: Predicting Performance in the White House*, 2d ed. (Englewood Cliffs, N.J.: Prentice-Hall, 1977).

6. Ibid., p. 14.

7. Joe McGinniss, *The Selling of the President 1968* (New York: Trident Press, 1969).

8. Ibid., pp. 26–27.

9. Ibid., p. 28.

10. Barber, *Presidential Character*, pp. 445–446.

11

Open Gate

The Eugene McCarthy campaign of 1968 was remarkable, in the tradition of Kefauver's efforts, but fundamentally and philosophically different in both motivation and execution. McCarthy's audacity and nerve went almost unnoticed at first. How could this gentle man stand up to the Texan president of the United States, to the bombast of the militants who branded as disloyal any questioning of America's defense of freedom in Southeast Asia? How dare he question the established political leadership up and down the line, to most of whom it had not occurred that the United States might be wrong in time of war! He went his lonely way, with scant support and little recognition, until suddenly attention was riveted on this candidate who would stop the war.

It was as if he did not want the presidency. He gave no signs of hungering for it. Yet he was in political life, a politician, and all politicians have some thirst for power and authority, and he himself had sought support for the vice-presidency four years earlier. The magnitude of his mission seemed to put the presidency, and the seeking of it, into a marvelous perspective where power and position did not matter so much anymore, except for the power of politics to change politics. Gene McCarthy was not a tough politician, yet he had given himself the toughest of political assignments.

He won in New Hampshire and in Wisconsin, jolting the Johnson administration. He gave faith to young people. He eventually was overpowered by the more ambitious, the more regular, and the more organized, but he proved that the nominating process within the system could be elevated to deadly use against the establishment and the political system.

He struck the spark that blew up the war, although it took a few more years, and he got the nation back to some sanity— that was his lasting contribution to the nation. He also made a lasting contribution to the American presidency in that he proved the path to the presidency was open, that open was good, and that it could and should be opened even more.

As we toy with the nominating process and procedures, change the rules to make them more responsive, representative, or deliberative, and as we reinforce party structure, we should always measure what we do by the standard of what the proposed changes would have done to Gene McCarthy in 1968. Rules and procedures will not be adequate or satisfactory unless they permit entry by a Gene McCarthy. In the history of presidential selection, there has been no finer hour. Nor is a system adequate that is incapable of giving a fair hearing to a Howard Baker or an Ed Muskie. It does not serve us well to cut off likely and promising candidates before we even know them.

There is another observation—a delicate one, a subjective one. George C. Wallace bullied his way into presidential politics by exploiting cynically and hypocritically the fears of racial prejudice. Later, when this strategy was no longer politically rewarding, he modified his speech to champion the alternative prejudices, as well as many of the understandable doubts and fears of people, but always maintaining the underlying assurance that he could be trusted because he had paid his dues to white supremacy.

"Welfare," "crime in the streets," and opposition to "busing, any busing," can become code words for racial prejudice. It is unthinkable that the political bosses who picked Stevenson, Roosevelt, and Hubert Humphrey or Thomas Dewey, Dwight D. Eisenhower, Alfred Landon, and Wendell Willkie would ever have picked George C. Wallace to be the standard bearer for either principal party. This does not suggest that many of Wallace's assertions and positions would not have been in agreement with their own thoughts, but they would have looked more deeply, more broadly, for the positive characteristics needed in the presidency. Wallace may have had them, but our presidential primary system didn't require him to display them. Yet if George Wallace had been smarter, or if he had understood the system, he might well have captured the Democratic nomination.

The open, binding primary is frequently susceptible to the emotional and demagogic negative appeal. Not many people vote, and if enough are stirred on a particular issue, they might easily follow the protest route. Maybe Wallace would have made a good president, but he never would have been picked by the party elders unless he told them more than he told the voters in the primaries. He could have been picked by the people—at least those who vote in primaries.

If we want a system that keeps the door always open for a Gene McCarthy, do we need some checkpoint that would permit a few more questions to be asked of a George Wallace?

12

Are Political
Parties Expendable?

Canada, modeled as it is on the centuries-old English system, finds the process for electing its chief executive far simpler than our devices and structures. Prime Minister Joe Clark, generally unknown to the Canadian public, had been tried and tested by his fellow party members in Parliament and selected as their leader, a little over three years before becoming prime minister, by a convention considerably different from conventions in the United States. When a new election gave his party a working majority, thin though it was, he was immediately called to form the government, and Prime Minister Pierre Trudeau stepped aside. However, Trudeau retained his seat in Parliament, since that is what he was running for, not the prime ministership.

Prime Minister Trudeau, then eleven years in that office, had on March 26, 1979, dissolved Parliament and called the election for May 22, 1979. Campaigning and electioneering lasted less than two months. The Canadian voters do not elect, at least not directly, their prime minister. They vote, in their respective districts, for 282 members of one of the houses of Parliament, the House of Commons, although obviously they know which candidate for prime minister they are indirectly supporting. In turn the party with a majority "elects" the prime minister, each party having already agreed on the "nomination," and the leader of the majority party becomes the prime minister.

On December 13, 1979, the Clark Government "fell," that is, it failed—by six votes—to carry a significant bill in Parliament.[1] Prime Minister Clark forthwith called a new election, and the voters and the delegates went back to the drawing board.

In that election, held on February 18, 1980, Trudeau's Liberal party picked up additional seats in Parliament, enough to give his party a clear majority, so he straightaway re-formed his government with himself as prime minister. Mr. Clark moved out but remained in Parliament, to which he had been reelected. His party had retained, in fact, its right to govern for only nine months. In the United States it takes much more than nine months to conduct a campaign for the presidency.

There are several apparent advantages the Canadians enjoy. The duration of the campaigning is limited. The leaders, the prime minister and prime minister-to-be, have been deliberately chosen as party leaders, generally well in advance of the election, by a convention system that tends to promote party solidarity.[2] There is almost always the alternative leader waiting, not in the wings, but on the floor of the House of Commons, participating daily in the affairs of the nation. That the Commonwealth nations almost always have strong and effective prime ministers is a compelling tribute to the parliamentary process of national leadership begun in the thirteenth century with the parliaments of Edward I. That a parliamentary nation can change governments, or reaffirm them, according to the national needs and the exigencies of the times, not waiting for the elapse of an inflexible term of years such as that more or less arbitrarily set for our government by the Constitution in 1789, is another apparent value.

Had the United States adopted the parliamentary system, we might speculate, Lyndon Johnson could have gracefully stepped aside in 1967 without waiting until we were forced to endure the ordeal of 1968. Richard Nixon need not have resigned; he could have "fallen." Perhaps at a low point in the summer of 1979 President Carter could have called new elections, either to be reaffirmed, as Prime Minister Clark had hoped to be, or to step aside for Howard Baker (or would it have been Representative John J. Rhodes?) waiting and working as minority leader.

The system of the British Commonwealth has endured because it almost invariably brings well-qualified and proven people to leadership. It has also endured, it must be argued, because it nurtures and is nurtured by a structure of political parties and because it is ideally suited to, and dependent upon, an essentially two-party system.[3]

The British system requires political party affiliations and loyalty to party. Otherwise, it could not work. Because our procedures can work, or appear for brief times to work, without much party loyalty or party affiliation, there is an eminent temptation to try to get along without effective party organizations. More likely, we will inadvertently but mortally wound political party concepts by attempting to charge parties with functions they cannot carry out while ignoring their true and successful function in history.

David Broder has written persuasively that we have already all but abandoned our faith in political parties to the disenchantment of society with the total of society.[4] To lose faith in political parties is to lose faith in our ability to make self-government work. The size of the nation and the complexity of the issues have made political parties necessary from the very time Alexander Hamilton and Thomas Jefferson squared off. Not to have had political parties, a position advocated by President George Washington, who hoped we could have a government without partisanship, would have meant a government without the discipline of opposition. It also would have meant a continual disruption of government by those people who disagreed with it but had no means of expression. In simplest terms, the development of political parties made our new form of self-government work.

Of those early days of the republic, it has been noted that "Secret societies, subversion, and defiance seemed the only course possible to many who disapproved of government policies, since an opposition party had yet to be formed, much less vindicated by popular opinion."[5] President Washington's instincts were generous and loving, but all the while Hamilton was molding together those people who would be Federalists and, by considering all others to be the enemy, creating a climate in which an opposition party was bound to rise. As Joseph Charles said, Washington "is to be blamed, not for allying himself with a party, but for not knowing that he had done so, and for denouncing those opposed to his party as opposed to the government."[6]

Not to have had political parties based on a wide range of issues and grounded on broad concepts or instinctive principles would have given us a hodgepodge of numerous special-interest groups intent on achieving a single or momentary goal at the expense of the general good. The United States is too large to settle its affairs by pure democracy, although our presidential nominating system often gives the impression that we have abandoned our belief in the republican principles of representative government. The United States has too many problems, activities, and concerns to abandon the coalescing force of major political parties.

Alexander Hamilton was not always consistent as an individual, but he was consistent as the leader of the emerging first party as he sought to bring together under one banner many people with a variety of interests, some or most of whom were self-serving and all of whom potentially shared with him a vision of what they wanted the government to do and the nation to be.[7] That is the function of a political party: to iron out differences, to reach acceptable compromises and adjustments, and to unify.

Our general malaise, disappointment, and disillusionment of the last decade or more have made us wary of political parties, political bosses, and, indeed, of politics itself. We have seen the political parties as closed shops and self-promoters, little concerned with the public good. The charges against the operators of political machinery are true sometimes but not most of the time, and the imperfections, like the imperfections in our other institutions, are correctable. The pyramid on the Great Seal, printed on every dollar bill, is incomplete and awaiting our faith in our capacity to keep on building. Of course political parties need to be shaped up and improved. What doesn't?

As we grope for ways to reaffirm our faith in our self-government, our nation, and ourselves, one starting point is the political party. David Broder established, impressively, I think, that "we can make government responsible and responsive again, only when we begin to use the political parties as they were meant to be used."[8] He warned that "the challenge facing our society is far more critical than most of us find comfortable to believe," unless we find some inspiration to "make political parties . . . the instrument of national self-renewal."[9]

Broder's book is an excellent defense of the party system. We must have, he stated,

> some institution that will sort out, weigh, and, to the extent possible, reconcile the myriad conflicting needs and demands of individuals, groups, interests, communities and regions in this diverse continental Republic; organize them for the contest for public office; and then serve as a link between the constituencies and the men chosen to govern. When the parties fill their mission well, they tend to serve both a unifying and a clarifying function for the country.[10]

Yet how many people in the United States are willing to believe that tenet? How many young people are firmly con-

113

vinced that politics and political parties are rotten to the core? How many respectable and otherwise responsible residents of our rife and sprawling suburbs have been heard to say glibly, "I vote for the man, not the party."

Did we not swarm to support Dwight D. Eisenhower, and does that not prove that political parties are unnecessary? Did not Jimmy Carter initially run successfully as one vaguely suspicious of both his political party and the government? History will say, accurately, that we needed Eisenhower, a man out of and therefore above partisan politics, to give us time to regroup and start anew. It should not be overlooked, however, that responsive agents of a political party in a convention picked Eisenhower for this perceived role. For all its shortcomings, that Republican Convention served the function of intelligent deliberation about as well as any convention in our time. The Republican party functioned well as a political party in 1952, as did the Democratic party. What has happened in both parties since 1952 has caused the upheaval of our faith in political parties. Perhaps, with due respect, President Carter's troubles with Congress demonstrated that we have a compelling need to revive our political parties and the conciliating and unifying force they have been known to provide.

Broder's case for the American political party includes making political parties again more a part of the presidential nominating process. It cannot be denied that we have gleefully attempted to bypass the party to give the inconstant voting public a stronger direct voice in the presidential nomination. That idea is commendable, but it is not the way to make self-government work. The 1964 Republican Convention and especially the 1968 Democratic Convention caused us to think parties thwarted the public will. We changed the rules. We opened up the parties. We "returned government to the people." Like a monkey's uncle we did!

We took the organization out of the process, and we thrust the job of unifying and organizing upon the individuals who

114

would seek the presidency. The two tasks are incompatible. There are many reasons for reviving political parties and, as Broder put it, for using political parties to renew our faith in our self-government. One starting point for such self-renewal is a return to the parties for improving the presidential nominating process.

The party should assert its superior and raw authority to approve or disapprove state laws setting various methods and time schedules for the selection of delegates, and the party should insist upon compliance with party guidelines as the entry fee to the convention floor. The parties are now buffeted and twisted by the whim of state legislators interested in provincial pretensions instead of goals that serve the nation in presenting the best-possible candidates to the voters.

That the party has this authority is a settled matter of law.[11] A party does not have the right to discriminate or to violate provisions of the Constitution, or to make or amend laws, but it does have the right otherwise to determine who can be a delegate to its conventions. By asserting this right, the party can set dates within which primaries might be held, can decide the limits of alternative methods for selecting delegates, and can define the kind of instructions and directions the delegates are to receive. A state should not be permitted to bind a delegate in a manner contrary to the will of the party. The party can also require affirmative action of various sorts to be observed in delegate selection. The power of the party prevails over state law to this limited but adequate extent, because the party decides which delegates can be seated at a convention.

Iowans cannot be blamed for enjoying the television attention they now receive. The legislators and governor of New Hampshire cannot be blamed for wanting to hold the first primary. The primary has given the people of that state a unique place in American politics. It brings in money for the merchants, motels, restaurants, and druggists who sell cold and flu medicines. Julian Scheer has reported on New Hampshire:

They love the spectacle. They love shaking hands. They love asking hard questions. They love joshing one another at the Grange
Hall. The activity here is unlike any other state, despite the obvious distortions: New Hampshire is a tiny state; it has no income
tax; it has fewer than 200,000 people;—it votes largely Republican; it has only a few delegates. The candidates ignore the facts
and still apply occult-like fervor toward winning here. . . . "We
have politics," says John Dole, "on every level. This is the ultimate. And we love the attention. We love being first. We love
everyone looking at New Hampshire. Why not? Besides, when else
do you hear about New Hampshire?"[12]

The political powers of California cannot be blamed for
wanting the attention that the last primary spot provides,
with the added sweetener of a state-mandated winner-take-
all rule. It helps them receive extra attention. Never mind
that the rule is undemocratic and unfair to the voters who
have cast a ballot for other candidates. Never mind that the
rule is contrary to the party philosophy that has been resist-
ing and eliminating unit rules for years at other levels and in
other places.

There is no force other than party determination that can
bring some sense to the jumble of state primaries, except
Congress, and congressional regulation is certainly not desirable. The parties can do it, and in 1978 the Democrats
took a hesitant step with the rules by setting the second
Tuesday in March of election year as the first date any primary
or first-tier caucus might be held and the second Tuesday of
June as the last date for such processes.[13] Thus the primaries
would be contained in a thirteen-week period. New Hampshire, on the front end, California, on the tail end, and
a few other states were granted a 1980 temporary exemp-
tion from the rule, although the rules provide that if there
are conflicts with existing state laws, "the State Party shall
take provable positive steps to bring the state law into compliance." The Democratic rules further provide that "A State
Party may be required to adopt and implement an alternative

Party-run delegate selection system which does not conflict with these rules, regardless of any provable positive steps the state may have taken."[14] There has been fair warning for 1984.

The Republican party rules provide that "All delegates and alternates shall be elected not later than thirty-five (35) days before the date of the first meeting of said national convention, unless otherwise provided by the laws of the state in which the election occurs."[15]

I write as one believing that the two-party system that evolved naturally during the first years of our republic has served us well and deserves to be renewed and refreshed in the service of the nation. I contend that the two parties can get on with an examination of ways they can make our presidential selection system a sounder and surer process of self-government. Their effort will work both ways. Generating the internal capacity to change the nominating process certainly will make the presidency stronger and more effective, and that accomplishment will make the parties stronger and more acceptable. It is an invitation the parties cannot afford to refuse.

Notes

1. "Casual Joe Takes a Fall," *Time*, 24 December 1979, p. 32.

2. See Carl Baar and Ellen Baar, "Party and Convention Organization and Leadership Selection in Canada and the United States," in *Perspectives on Presidential Selection*, ed. Donald R. Matthews (Washington, D.C.: Brookings Institution, 1973), pp. 49–84.

3. Not always just two. In the 1980 elections, the Canadian Liberal party received 49 percent of the vote, Joe Clark's Progressive Conservative party received 28 percent, and the New Democrats got 18 percent.

4. See David S. Broder, *The Party's Over: The Failure of Politics in America* (New York: Harper & Row, 1971).

5. Joseph Charles, *The Origins of the American Party System* (New York: Harper & Row, 1956), p. 42.

6. Ibid., p. 44.

7. Ibid., 7–36.

8. Broder, *The Party's Over*, p. xvi.

9. Ibid., p. xi.

10. Ibid., pp. xx–xxi.

11. Cousins v. Wigoda, 95 S.Ct. 541 (1975), and O'Brien v. Brown, 92 S.Ct. 2718 (1972).

12. Julian Scheer, "New Hampshire Looks Candidates in the Eye," *The News and Observer,* Raleigh, North Carolina, 27 February 1980, p. 4.

13. *Delegate Selection Rules for the 1980 Democratic National Convention* by John C. White, Chairman (Washington, D.C.: Democratic National Committee, 1978), p. 10.

14. Ibid., p. 16.

15. *Rules Adopted by the 1976 Republican National Convention* (Kansas City, Mo.: Lowell Press, 1976), p. 15.

13

Primaries Unlimited

To suggest a diminishing role for the primaries is a skittish undertaking. Yet the bald reality is that the primary exercise is now madness. We have reformed ourselves into a primary maze that is chaotic and confusing, so costly as to dissuade most good possible candidates from even trying, and subject to massive media misinterpretation. Primaries additionally give the voters only one choice when in fact most primaries are held when reasonable voters might be satisfied with more than one of the candidates, especially in the earlier primaries.*

About 75 percent of the delegates were selected by primaries in 1980. Polls repeatedly show that people overwhelmingly approve of primaries. Yet for all this approval, it is beyond doubt that we should "do something" about the primaries. Certainly we do not want to do away with all primaries. They do serve as a safeguard against entrenched party leadership.

---

*See the Appendix for an interesting idea, an article by Steven J. Brams entitled "Approval Voting: A Practical Reform for Multicandidate Elections." It is not my recommendation at this time that this system be generally adopted, but it is promising enough for the parties to encourage several states to act as public laboratories by trying it.

They do serve as a safety valve for dissatisfaction—witness the McGovern campaign, which permitted millions to express a desire to end the Vietnam War. Primaries do give an opportunity for far more people to feel they have some part in the selection. To do away with primaries would appear to be taking something away from the people, and it would be.

> The proliferation of primaries in the last decade has been principally the outgrowth of Democratic reform rules, written and rewritten since the party's tumultuous 1968 convention to increase grass-roots participation in the delegate selection process.
>
> However, many party leaders are beginning to feel the growth in primaries has gone too far, creating a nominating system that emphasizes candidates' personal campaign organizations and media advertising.[1]

A Democratic party report in 1978 included a thoughtful discussion of this unanticipated change, pointing out the need "to bring some order into the currently chaotic primary system."[2] The report states, "Others have advocated decreasing, in some way, the impact that primaries have in the nominating process."[3] Still "others have suggested that improved standards be developed for the kinds of primaries that are allowed to send delegates to the convention."[4]

Beyond the chaos, a great danger in the primary system is that it promotes, indeed, insists on, a superficial exercise in the crucial task of selecting the leader of the free world. Even governors who are nominated in primaries get closer scrutiny, for the facts relative to record and qualifications are closer at hand for examination by the voters, and most states require a clear majority or a runoff election. Besides, we can afford to take a chance on getting a bad governor here and there, but the president should be selected with the greatest care and concern.

Those people who watch presidential primary campaigns have to be dismayed and distressed with this all-American carnival. In most cases we see a media blitz. Television spots, slick advertising, and attention-seeking slogans or antics may not always turn the trick, but they help build cynicism. Irrelevant issues that have emotional appeal get undue attention. Minor gaffes get magnified by too quick reporting. All is superficial. Maybe neither George Romney nor Edmund Muskie should have been president (although there was much to recommend both), but it is disgraceful that our process is so fragile and flimsy that they were ridiculed out of contention for nonsensical reasons, mostly by the emphasis provided by the news media commentators and editors. One used the wrong figure of speech in telling the truth about the deceit of our generals in Vietnam; the other was cashiered by an expression of understandable anger accompanied by an alleged few tears.

In a primary campaign it is difficult to get beyond a few slogans, so the press can hardly be blamed for picking up on the antics and the gaffes. There is just not much opportunity for serious public debate about presidential issues. Great interest can be generated about who thinks what about abortion, one of the most visible issues in several states in 1976 and the only lively exchange in the 1980 Anderson-Reagan debate, but that issue hardly has very much to do with the qualifications needed in the presidency.

The one-issue people generally come out to vote in the primaries, both to demand promises from the candidates and to vote for or against on the basis of gun control, the Equal Rights Amendment, or whatever single siren might be luring them. The candidates, understandably, respond in an effort to piece together enough fragments to make a decent showing, and they try to avoid making even a small segment mad. The candidates know they are surfing along on a bathtub tide, that if they "wipe out" they will not drown; but that matters little, for the herdlike chants of press and public will declare them drowned.

Not only does campaigning for the primaries generally have little to do with the qualifications for the presidency of the United States of America, it obscures the important questions, and it tempts the press to dwell on the obvious instead of digging for the essential. The candidates cannot be blamed. They are contending in a system they did not create, and we should expect them to play according to the rules even if the rules make little sense to them. They know from bitter experience or observation that the headlines and the newsbreaks the next day and weeks will dwell, not on records, achievements, character, important issues, or general approach to our national problems, but on a numbers game of who got what percentage of the vote measured against what percentage was claimed by or attributed to others. Foreigners think this is a ridiculous way to elect a leader, but we seem to like it. We are giving every citizen a voice in the elections, we say.

In campaigns for the presidential nomination, we have collectively allowed ourselves to act like children who play a game in which one spins around rapidly about six times and then looks at the world. The child comes out of the dizziness in a moment, but the voters never get their eyes uncrossed. Whether the voters spin themselves or are spun by the pollsters and the press makes little difference for the nation that must live or die, prosper or perish, by decisions made while in such a dazed and disoriented condition.

Jules Witcover,[5] an unusually good reporter and writer, in giving his readers a view of what he observed, used a quarter of a page in an edition of some 328,612 copies (the equivalent of four young pine trees) to tell excitedly about the possible dire results of George Bush's refusal in New Hampshire to debate with anyone but Reagan. "The big question is whether the impact will be negative and prompt enough to make a difference at the polls tomorrow." Because, he reported, the "Boston Globe's final poll released yesterday had Bush leading Reagan by only a percentage point, 35 to 34, among Republican voters." That the argument about the debate might have had a significant influence is indeed disturbing. Witcover went on, a pine tree later, to observe, "whether the whole flap will win over enough new support for Reagan—or cause enough leakage in Bush's backing—to produce a Reagan victory and a Bush loss by tomorrow, is the intriguing short-run question."[6] Short run, indeed! Is the future leadership of a great nation to be measured by whether one candidate or the other got 35 percent or 34 percent, or even 50 percent in an early primary in a very small state? To a logical person sitting down in a rocking chair, smoking a pipe and reflecting about the situation, all that flap would not make very much difference, should hardly be judged as winning or losing in any event, and certainly could hardly have anything at all to do with the qualifications for the presidency of the United States. Why, indeed, should the rest of the nation give a damn what the voters of unique, delightful New Hampshire do?

Pogo, erstwhile presidential candidate, with all his wonderful satire, could not begin to draw a landscape so distorted as the one we spin ourselves into seeing every four years when we set about to choose our leader. "Is something wrong?" asked the husband whose wife returned home to find him sitting on the kitchen floor playing jackrocks while the sink remained full of dirty dishes.

Republican Senator Bob Packwood of Oregon, sponsor of legislation requiring regional primaries, has declared that "No decision of this magnitude is made with so little logic." Our primary exercise "now resembles more a snowball racing downhill than a rational, humane method designed to choose our leader."[7]

It is possible for a candidate to arrive at the convention with a majority of legally pledged votes without the party members or the general public knowing very much about him. It is fair to say this situation occurred in the cases of Goldwater and McGovern, and even Carter.

The primaries also simplify the party's task, and define its choice, by eliminating some candidates before the convention meets. In fact, while a series of election victories will not guarantee a nomination, it is almost certain that a series of defeats will remove an aspirant from any serious consideration. In recent years, Wendell Willkie, Estes Kefauver and Hubert Humphrey have abandoned their campaigns after defeats in primary elections.[8]

So have Robert Dole, Howard Baker, George Bush, Henry Jackson, and many another good man.

The primaries, however, are not all bad, not at all. They permit an assault on the establishment, when needed. They force candidates to face the voters and to display their agility in dealing with the public, an important characteristic for both a party nominee, who must carry the party banner in the general election, and a president, who must communicate and educate. Perhaps of greater importance, open political parties and presidential primaries provide an outlet for dissent and dissatisfaction, and for a feeling by the ordinary nonpolitical citizen that he or she is not cut off from the important process of selecting a presidential candidate. It is true, as David Broder wrote, that "millions of Americans now feel they have lost control of government,"[9] and to the extent that primaries afford an opportunity to gain a sense of participation, they have to be judged beneficial. The task of the party is to provide access to even more citizens, to enhance the feeling of belonging and influencing, so if there are changes to be made they should be for the purpose of making primaries more serious and useful. How might that be done? How, indeed?

For the caucus states much the same might be said. The Winograd Report observed, "The Commission in no way feels that caucus delegate selection is a less legitimate delegate selection procedure than primary selection. Both systems have inherent strengths and weaknesses, and the question of which system is better for use in particular states is a decision best made by the state party and not by direction of the National Party."[10] Alan Baron thinks the Iowa vote in 1980, for all its misplaced media emphasis, was encouraging.

Iowa party members, he wrote, came to the caucuses "because—for the first time—Iowans regarded caucuses as 'primaries,' rather than 'party meetings.' "[11] What are the implications of that change?

"But in states with open precinct caucuses, a hard-fought struggle on the local precinct level can all too easily result in caucus packing, bearing no relation to actual political sentiment in the precinct."[12] That was the opinion of the Hughes Commission,[13] which recommended, as one safeguard, an adaptation of Connecticut's town primary system used in selection of delegates to the national conventions. "A primary election between the nominated slate chosen by the caucus and the challenging one in Connecticut may be obtained when five percent of the enrolled Democrats in the town sign a petition calling for a primary. In Connecticut this year, thirty-one primary challenges were invoked and nine changed the results."[14]

Neither system, of course, is precisely representative. Those people who are motivated to come out to vote in a primary election are about half the percentage of those who vote in a general election, and the turnout in the latter is embarrassingly smaller than it should be. People who are motivated to attend the caucuses constitute an even smaller number. In the case of a caucus, perhaps more than in a primary state, the emphasis is on thorough organization and getting the eligible party members to the caucus at the appointed time and place. Party rules make it possible for any party member to attend a caucus (there are varying determinants of party membership), but few actually attend except the "party regulars," plus some people recruited by the candidates and their workers. Recruitment abilities are admirable traits, but more applicable to football than to the presidency. (But then we are much more thorough in examining the qualifications of our football coaches.) The candidate who gets the most supporters to attend a caucus wins the most delegates. It is somewhat disturbing to contemplate that those people who attend come, not to join the party council in serious deliberation of who should lead our nation, but rather with pledges made and minds made up in advance.

The caucus method usually has several tiers. The first is the precinct; the next, the county and sometimes the congressional district; and then, the state convention. Party rules generally preserve the proportional support throughout and prohibit the unit rule at any tier. These improvements provide a fair reflection of the diligence with which each candidate has worked and should add to the sense of usefulness of all who participate.

The Winograd Report noted that "proponents of the caucus system argue that the quality of participation in caucuses is superior to the quality of participation in primaries. Participants must attend a caucus meeting and participate in debate." Also, "caucuses can be a powerful tool for involving more people in the party organization. In states where the caucuses have functions other than delegate selection, such as the drafting of a state party platform . . . the caucus system promotes party unity and recruits workers."[15] This idea is possible, and promising, but the evidence is slim.

Opposition, the report continues, is generally "on the grounds that the people who participate in it are the same old 'courthouse gang' and are thus unrepresentative of voters in the electorate," but that argument is somewhat diminished because the new party reform rules "have made the present day caucuses different from the party-dominated caucuses of the past. This probably explains why there are no significant differences between delegates from caucuses and primary states."[16] (That's disheartening!)

The selection of delegates by party members in a small district by district elections is another method of choosing delegates, used separately or in conjunction with a primary election. For two examples, it is instructive to look at Illinois and Texas. This approach is sometimes disparagingly referred to as a "loophole" in the Democratic rule requiring "fair reflection of presidential preferences," but the new rules prohibit the winner-take-all provision that was most objectionable.[17]

In Illinois there is a nonbinding, advisory-only preferential primary held on the same day the national convention delegates and alternates are elected. The delegates are elected by congressional districts, and the total number, with some at-large slots reserved, is divided equally among the twenty-four districts. In 1980 the Democrats elected 179 delegates; the Republicans, 102. Candidates for national convention delegate must file a statement of candidacy and a petition signed by a specific number of the party electors in a congressional district. One petition may cover any number of candidates. Each candidate for delegate must also file a declaration of presidential preference or indicate an uncommitted position. The candidates receiving the highest number of votes are elected from each district. The vote is not by presidential candidate slate, although delegate slates are filed in most of the districts.

In 1980 in Texas the Republicans held a nonbinding preferential primary; the Democrats held no primary. Both parties elected delegates by congressional district. A slate of three was nominated for each district with the remainder at large statewide, all by a statutory procedure, but in effect they were slated by the presidential candidates. If a presidential candidate receives more than 50 percent of the district vote, that candidate gets all three delegates; if less, delegates are allocated by a statutory formula. The same procedure applies for the statewide delegates. The elected delegates are bound by state statute to the presidential candidate who slated them for at least the first two ballots. The voters mark their ballots for the presidential slate; the names of the delegates do not appear on the ballots.

This approach to the election of delegates could be modified and safeguarded in a manner to assure openness, participation, and fairness. It could be a middle ground between the advantages of the primary and the advantages of the caucus procedure. It might bring out more voters since delegate-candidates would be campaigning among their neighbors and the results would be visible and significant to the voters.

A disadvantage is that unless balanced slates are presented by the candidates, there is a possibility that not as many women and minority members will be selected as delegates. On the other hand, if districts were one-delegate districts, there could be as many as six such Democratic delegate districts in every congressional district, almost five Republican, and that might get the selection down to truly representative conditions, and also a fair total of women and minorities might be elected. This is a promising thought, if gerrymandering could be avoided.

There have been suggestions that the ideal approach would be to adopt a national primary or to set one day on which all state primaries would be held. These ideas have been translated into numerous bills introduced into Congress, and there are vigorous proponents available to argue the case. It appears that all of the disadvantages of the present primary system would continue except for the method of campaigning by the candidates, but many new difficulties would result as well.

It is not the purpose of this study to deal in any depth with this question, because it would require a drastic conceptual reform fraught with uncertainties, or so it seems to me, and therefore, as I have pondered this possibility over a number of years, I am inclined to rest my case by calling four witnesses. The National Democratic Convention in 1976 passed the following resolution.

Section 5. Resolved further that this Convention, recognizing the Responsibility of our National Party to provide for our Presidential nominating process, urges the U.S. Congress to refrain from intervening in these Party affairs unless and until the National Party requests legislative assistance, and in no case should Congress legislate in any manner which is in derogation of the right of a National Party to mandate its own affairs.[18]

President Harry S. Truman had this to say:

> The convention system has its faults, of course, but I do not know of a better method for choosing a presidential nominee. There has been a great deal of talk regarding the need of a presidential primary, but there is not a man in the country who could afford the expenses of both a primary and a campaign. The physical effort alone is no small consideration. In theory, it sounds plausible, but the great population centers of the country would have virtual control of the nomination for President. Yet it has been my experience that the "country boys" sometimes know more about the political needs of the country than the experts from the big city.[19]

The distinguished Commission on the Democratic Selection of Presidential Nominees issued a report adopted by the 1968 National Democratic Convention. Among many other things, it concluded that "The Commission believes that a national primary system for picking presidential nominees does *not* promise a complete corrective for the undemocratic aspects of current nominating procedures and that such a proposal if adopted would likely prove a cure more dangerous than the disease."[20]

Dwight D. Eisenhower, in *Reader's Digest*, July 1966, wrote:

> I am not among those who wish to abolish the nominating conventions in favor of a national primary. . . . There are, moreover, compelling arguments against a national primary. In most Presidential years at least two primary elections would be necessary. With perhaps four or five men seeking the nomination in each party, it is unlikely any one of them—except an incumbent President—could win a majority vote on the first round. Unless we nominated by plurality, which certainly is not desirable, a runoff would be necessary. All this would prolong the selection

129

of candidates. . . . Furthermore . . . only wealthy men could
normally run for the Presidency . . . and I certainly do not think
we should close the door to any man of integrity and ability
simply because he cannot afford to run.[21]

Susan Furniss has suggested an interesting, and workable,
alternative to a national nominating primary. It appears to
me that it would be difficult to effect such a reverse in established thinking, but it is worth consideration, and the idea is
an example of the kind of creative searching the major parties should conduct.

She would have delegates selected by a tiered (generally
precinct, district, state) system. The delegates would attend
the national party convention unbound, but perhaps generally
instructed. The convention would nominate candidates for
the national party primary. A candidate's name would be
placed on the primary ballot if he or she had received 30 (or
some other) percent of the convention votes. The winner of
the national primary would be the party nominee for the
November general election. The party structure thus would
be responsible for nominating candidates who would run in a
national primary, so there would be a level of deliberation
and thoughtful consideration before the primaries, instead
of the other way around. This procedure would not prevent
candidates from independent or third parties from running
in the general election. It would bring order to the concept
of primaries.

Furniss summarized, "The plan does a number of things to
strengthen the party. (1) The activists make the first cut,
(2) the convention deliberates and further refines the field,
and (3) the broader party electorate makes the final decision."[22]

There is a long history of fascination with presidential
primaries, and the parties dare not talk of abolishing them.
The parties can change, however, the maze to a system and
convert the chaos to a recognizable purpose.

Notes

1. Rhodes Cook, "Presidential Primaries Reach Record Level," *Congressional Quarterly*, 4 August 1979, p. 1609.

2. *Openness, Participation and Party Building: Reforms for a Stronger Democratic Party* by Morley A. Winograd, Chairman, Commission on Presidential Nomination and Party Structure (Washington, D.C.: Democratic National Committee, 1978), p. 31.

3. Ibid, p. 30.

4. Ibid, p. 31.

5. *Washington Star* political editor.

6. Jules Witcover, "Rancor Grips Close GOP Race After Debate," *Washington Star*, 25 February 1980, p. A3.

7. Cook, "Presidential Primaries Reach Record Level," p. 1610.

8. Gerald Pomper, *Nominating the President* (Evanston, Ill.: Northwestern University Press, 1963), p. 110.

9. David S. Broder, *The Party's Over: The Failure of Politics in America* (New York: Harper & Row, 1971), p. xvii.

10. *Openness, Participation and Party Building*, p. 30.

11. Alan Baron, "Inside: Analysis of the Democratic and Republican Presidential Races—and the November Election," *Baron Report*, 23 January 1980.

12. *Congressional Record*, 114:31550.

13. Chairman, Harold Hughes, governor of Iowa; vice-chairman, Donald M. Fraser, U.S. House of Representatives.

14. See *Congressional Record*, 114:31550–51.

15. *Openness, Participation and Party Building*, p. 29.

16. Ibid., pp. 29–30.

17. Ibid., p. 6.

18. Ibid., pp. 31–32.

19. Harry S. Truman, *Memoirs*, vol. 2, *Years of Trial and Hope* (Garden City, N.Y.: Doubleday & Company, 1956), p. 204.

20. *Congressional Record*, 114:31545.

21. Dwight D. Eisenhower, "Our National Nominating Conventions Are a Disgrace," *Reader's Digest*, July 1966, pp. 76–77.

22. Letter to author, May 12, 1980. Susan Furniss is former professor of political science, Colorado State University, and presently director of the Colorado office of Senator Gary Hart.

14

Thinking Delegates

Radical change in the way we choose presidential candidates is required if we are to maintain our leadership as a self-governing people. "Radical" means a fresh attitude. It also means giving up certain perceived rights. The latter will be more difficult. It is easier to change attitudes than to be unselfish and objective in reassessing rights and preferred positions.

Robert S. Strauss, former chairman of the Democratic National Committee and chairman of the Carter/Mondale Presidential Committee, had this to say: "Perhaps because of my role in the current campaign, this election has taught me more than any other that the methods used to pick a President are flawed, and in need of reform."[1]

Everyone will agree that we must find ways to renew faith in the American presidential nominating process. We must simultaneously reaffirm the essential nature of American political parties and work for the improvement of the two-party system. Like horse and carriage, love and marriage, we can't have one without the other.

Jules Abels, in a book entitled *The Degeneration of Our*

Presidential Election, with the subtitle *A History and Analysis of an American Institution in Trouble*, asks a troubling question: "The basic premise of democracy is an informed electorate. In its simplest terms, we may well ask today, can the people govern if they do not know what it is all about?"[2] Can we, he asked ten journalists who have observed political campaigns for many years, put substance "into the Presidential campaign, so that a voter can make his choice on more than snap or superficial judgment?" "Hardly," was the general answer. There is too much indifference, ignorance, lack of rational thinking, and inclination to react rather than to think.

"The consensus of political writers in this canvass . . . is that our Presidential election is in trouble," Abels reported, and then asserted, "We can throw up our hands and say that the present situation is due to inherent flaws in the democratic processes. On the other hand, we can make a try to do something about it."[3]

If I have not established the point that our two-party system must be preserved and enhanced, then we do not proceed from here on common ground. The development of a rational nominating process will improve the two-party system, will strengthen each party, and ultimately increase the people's confidence in political parties to perform their essential functions in self-government. True, such a development is not all the parties must do to survive. They need to work in states and localities to educate and organize, but it is essential for their survival and continuation that the Republican and Democratic parties assume anew the responsibility for presidential nominations.

I propose that the parties take charge, resolutely, of improving the presidential nominating process, not leaving the possibility of change to congressional action or to luck. The Republican party and the Democratic party, instead of bemoaning the possibility that "the party is over," can grasp the chance to save themselves and the American presidency.

134

Those who fear political bosses, and therefore would weaken political parties, might be reminded that the parties are open and leadership positions are available for those who seek them. Those people who would be cynical might also ponder the historical fact that political leaders as bosses are a thing of the past—but they were not all that bad in helping pick American presidents.

There are certain matters not embraced by my set of suggestions. The electoral college system is one. It may or may not cry out for reform, but it has little to do presently with who is nominated for the presidency. It is also not necessary to consider here party rules that apply to the apportionment of delegates to the various states, the total number of delegates and alternates, or convention housekeeping rules. It is not even necessary to consider affirmative action rules and processes for challenges, since the parties are constantly modifying those procedures.

It is appropriate to state that I believe in the usefulness of state presidential primaries. I also believe in the usefulness of caucuses. The national nominating convention, I contend, is fundamental, a "last clear chance" for deliberate and considered action, and should be preserved. The key, in fact, is to design the convention to be a deliberative body.

The nomination of a president should not be carried out in a sterile cage. Our presidency is a dynamic element of a dynamic democracy, and the presidential nomination cannot and should not be reduced to computerized efficiency. The process of seeking the American president is inexorably interwoven with the adventure of a democratic people who are not at all satisfied with what we have already remarkably achieved in fulfilling the yearnings and insistencies of the human spirit. It would not do, nor would it be possible, for us to adopt the British system. The wild, exciting, emotional characteristics of party activity in the selection of presidential nominees are not to be abandoned simply because the process is not orderly and predictable. Adventure, in human terms, is more vital than orderliness.

Therefore, the reshaping of presidential nominating procedures should not be attempted with an attitude of retrenchment. Procedures should exude confidence in the people and in their capacity for self-government. That is America's indispensable message to the world and our immutable obligation to our heritage. Any proposal also should have the advantage of being amenable to easy amendment, change, or fine-tuning from convention to convention so that nothing is to be locked in for very long, which should be true of all important democratic institutions.

There are some characteristics we should define as desirable in the nominating process, and we should attempt to shape the process to fit those characteristics. Judith H. Parris, writing in 1972 as a research associate in the Brookings Governmental Studies Program, backed up by a bipartisan advisory council and an additional group of scholars, set forth carefully considered "Criteria for Evaluating Conventions."[4] Her conclusions are a good starting point for renewed deliberations in the 1980s. Parris included (1) fairness, (2) the extent of democracy, (3) efficiency, (4) reasonableness, (5) consensus, and (6) legitimacy as the desirable criteria for the convention procedures. The same criteria apply also to the total nominating process.

Fairness, she pointed out, means the convention rules "should not discriminate systematically against any group." Except that the system now discriminates against political and public leadership, this criterion has already been achieved by the two parties, or can be with easy adjustments. Certainly it is an accepted proposition by both parties. It requires, and will receive, constant vigilance. It does not, or should not, mean that we artificially place people in positions as a token of our fairness.

Fairness, however, also means that rules should be applied regardless of who gains or loses, and they "must not only *be* fair, they must *look* fair,"[5] because television is watching.

Under our present procedures, especially in the Democratic candidate-controlled setting, this criterion of fairness cannot be achieved, for the candidate with the votes will interpret the rules to his or her advantage. Would George McGovern's managers at the 1972 convention, with a majority of delegates in hand, have voted to sustain the California unit rule if McGovern had received 39 percent of the vote and Hubert H. Humphrey 44 percent, instead of the other way around? Of course not. McGovern's people would have fought it, sanctimoniously declaring that the unit rule denied democracy. Which it does! Certainly, if they had held the votes, Humphrey's people would have taken the same action. We should seek to design a convention that would make such decisions objectively if the process is to achieve credibility.

Parris noted that "the new thrust is toward diversity, while the old impulse was toward unity," so "democracy in procedures may clash headlong with the convention's traditional objectives of efficiency, legitimacy, reasonableness, and unity as a means of victory."[6] So be it. Openness is more desirable than efficiency. But what about unity and victory? And legitimacy—belief by the people?

She did not dwell on the delegates' opportunity for deliberation, careful examination of candidates' qualifications, and concern for the broad and future issues, all of which are elements put to disadvantage under the present rules. When she wrote, the parties had not abandoned these elements. Parris did conclude that a "restructured convention" is what we need and that "the short answer . . . is that the convention should be a representative and sometimes deliberative body, of which both party activists and party-in-the-electorate are vital organs."[7] This answer is sound, but it is not simple.

Parris thought that "the delegates should reflect accurately the candidate preferences of their rank-and-file constituencies. Hence they should be selected on that basis."[8] We have learned that this principle cannot be achieved, in the sense she suggested and subsequent rules require, if we also want the

137

delegates to be a "deliberative body." It is an incongruity to expect a delegate to be an automatic convention vote for a candidate and at the same time serve as a member of a deliberative group reflecting the views of rank-and-file constituencies. How in the world we do get around that dilemma?

Walter Lippmann wrote that

> Washington believed that the people should rule. But he did not believe that *because* the people ruled, there would be freedom, justice, and good government. He did not believe that the sovereign people, any more than the royal sovereigns whom they succeeded, could be trusted with absolute power. . . .
>
> He did not believe in what has become the prevailing ideology of democracy—that whatever the mass of the people happen to think they want must be accepted as the right. "I am sure," he once wrote to John Jay, "that the mass of citizens in these United States *mean well*, and I firmly believe that they will always *act well*, whenever they can obtain a right understanding of matters."[9]

This commentary is precisely applicable today to presidential primaries. Lippmann's point was that the Constitution intended that the will of the people is to be, not the first idea that pops out of their heads on a particular spring morning, but an expression that has been given some time and distance to mature and be refined. That is why we have representative government with checks and balances.

The founders of the American republic, Lippmann observed, "invented devices for balancing the constituencies and delaying their decisions. They sought to make the people safe for democracy. What they meant to do every civilized people has to do."[10] In the vast United States pure democracy is not as reliable as representative democracy.

It seems to me we are mixed up on what constitutes a representative body, and it is necessary to resolve that confusion. The real test must be whether all segments of a voting constituency have full and free opportunity and encouragement to vote for the representative they choose to vote for.

138

The manner of selecting "representative" delegates to the national conventions is the crux of legitimate dissatisfaction with the nominating process. The new rules made a fundamental change; the candidates, not the constituents, pick the delegates. The way this selection is made seems so reasonable and obvious that we can't believe it is wrong. But it is.

The system, in fact, is fooling us if it requires a slate of sample citizens from specified segments of society, picked or approved by a partisan, to attend a convention on the pretense that the segments, and the whole, are therefore properly represented. Is a woman mayor any less representative of the male population of Chicago or San Francisco because of her sex? The real test is not what the mayor is, but whether everyone—male and female, regardless of color, national origin, or whatever—had the chance to vote without obstruction when she was elected. She represents, finally, every citizen. Does a young and struggling black lawyer elected to the state legislature not represent all of his or her constituents, including those in different income groups? Is the Congress of the United States less than democratic and representative because "racial, sexual, age, and income groups" are not "in proportion to their share" of the constituency? Although it might lack the quality it would have if more women were members, Congress is certainly representative as that word is properly defined. There are not more women in Congress, it seems to me, because not enough women are running for Congress; when women get ready to move in, they will.

We cannot have a convention delegate who is the representative of a presidential candidate and at the same time the representative of the delegate's broad constituency. This point is radical. To make a delegate serve the voter instead of a candidate, the way we used to do it, is, in today's climate, oddly radical and will require a radical change.

It will take some jolting of our established notions to acknowledge that a delegate to a presidential nominating convention should be selected on the basis of the constituency's confidence in her or him to be representative, honest, and intelligent, regardless of all other considerations—including sex, age, color, bank account, or commitment to a particular presidential candidate. The bedrock difference is whether we prefer that a delegate go to the convention to think and act for us or as a messenger to vote for a particular candidate, as we have rather inexactly and perhaps prematurely instructed, and to vote on other questions and platform issues as that candidate might signal. What are the advantages of sending uninstructed delegates, and how dare we ignore the sovereign vote of the people in committing that delegate to vote as we did—or as some of us did?

Our present procedure for nominating presidential candidates is a process of elimination. "This candidate," we and the press observe, "cannot make it past New Hampshire." Or, "He will be gone by Illinois." A process of elimination is all right for deciding the NCAA basketball championship, but it hardly serves well the American republic. It would have benefited us if Howard Baker could have been looked at more carefully, but he did not turn properly at the first flag so he was ruled out of the race. That type of elimination is all right for downhill slalom skiing, but adopting it for the presidential process is taking the country downhill in a different and more deadly use of that word. It might be that the thinking delegates would not have chosen Baker, but that is not the point. Some representative group of Republicans would have had an opportunity to look at him in comparison with all other possibilities. As it is, when the looking time arrives almost all of the possible candidates have gone home.

Eastern Airlines, when looking for a president, could go outside its ranks and pick an astronaut as its chief executive. The Stanford Graduate School of Business could reach into the business world for its dean. Duke University could look at every basketball coach in the country before making an offer to the one it perceived would best serve Duke. The

Methodist Church can look at every preacher in the juris-
diction, and at others who are not preachers, when the time
comes to elect a bishop. The political party delegates to the
national nominating conventions can look at only one or two
survivors who have run a crazy obstacle course. I am in favor
of delegates who can look at the full field, and even beyond
the full field, in order to pick the best possible presidential
candidate. Of course that is a radical thought. We need and
must have a radical change.

Adlai Stevenson and Charles Evans Hughes would never
have been candidates had they been required to gear up for a
present-day campaign survival exercise, and yet they were,
with some reluctance, willing to have their names and qualifications considered by a thoughtful convention of delegates.
We need a process that makes it easier for such people to be
considered and that makes it possible to seek out those who
are highly qualified, to draft the man or woman who could
best serve the nation. A burning desire to be president, a
necessary trait under today's rules, is not the most admirable
characteristic for a president, but we have made it the most
essential.

Affirmative action is a principle we espouse for businesses,
universities, and associations, but political parties do not
apply the principle of affirmative action to presidential selection. They reach out and encourage voters to participate in
party activities and delegate selection; they advertise and
interview and seek a wide range of applicants for office staffs.
But there is no affirmative action search for presidential candidates, and applicants are discouraged by the very procedures.

The vote of a constituency, be it in the voting booth or in
a caucus, is typically not very clear-cut. There will be in the
early stages of the presidential campaign a number of candidates, and a clear majority vote for any single candidate is
unlikely. We have no way of indicating a second choice;
obviously the person with the second-largest vote is not
necessarily a constituency's second choice. The person in

141

fourth place could be almost everybody's second choice. It is also true that the average voter does not see much finality about the primary or caucus election, and he or she could be voting with less-serious determination than when casting a vote in the general election. A greater danger in giving instructions too early is that if the opportunity were provided for the delegate and the constituents to learn more about the qualifications and characteristics of the candidates, they might all change their minds.

Ideally we should want a delegate who is honorable and uninstructed, but aware of and responsive to the feelings of the constituency and accountable to the constituency. Accountability cannot be effective, some would argue, because a delegate is a one-shot representative and cannot be voted out because of a miscalculation of the constituency's desires. I disagree.

Walter Cronkite has argued that "With the advent of television, the very purpose of the convention has been broadened. Before, it was a relatively private meeting to determine party policy and select those candidates the delegates and their leaders thought had the best chance to lead the party to victory." Television coverage makes the delegate

> less responsive to political manipulation and more to the loud, clear voice of his constituents back home than he was before television. Because of television's full coverage the folks back home are just as conversant with the issues, the men, and even the back-room deals, as is the delegate, and they let him know their feelings with a constant flood of telegrams and telephone calls. He is more the people's representative than ever before.[11]

That was written before the new rules. Now it does no good to wire or call; the delegate belongs to the candidate. But this situation can be changed.

My argument is that the delegates have to go home, where they will be called on to explain their votes, and that the vast majority of those people who manage to become delegates will want other honors and political opportunities. Even so, the question is, Do we want to trade the messenger concept for the deliberative delegate concept?

Those of us who have over the years sought fairer representation for women and members of minorities might well be apprehensive that abandoning candidate-slating would decrease the degree of "representation" those groups have attained. I would be willing to bet that this would not be so. Women and members of minorities are increasingly winning public office, and they could present a particularly appealing case in a delegate election.

If perception and other interests keep many of the women and minorities from full-time political office,[12] the same would not apply to seeking a delegate's slot. Such a position is, as a matter of fact, an ideal point of entry into political activity. In any event, would not women and minorities, somewhat favored in the recent past by special preference, find it more satisfying to go as duly elected, independent, responsible, and responsive delegates? Admittedly that idea requires a long-range and unselfish view.

I would suggest to the political parties that the process of nominating presidential candidates can be improved immeasurably by adherence to three broad principles. Rules and procedures might vary, but the principles must be observed.

FIRST PRINCIPLE: Send *thinking delegates* to the national conventions. This means we must elect delegates who are uninstructed or, at least, not irrevocably bound.

It would be ideal to elect delegates from the smallest district possible, preferably one delegate per district. The party rules could be changed simply to require that the delegates be elected individually, on the basis of the confidence the voters have in that person, just as we elect school board members, state representatives, and other public officials. Then we would have going to the convention a real, live, thinking person instead of the equivalent of a blip on a computer tape slated by a candidate's staff and programmed to vote just so and no other way.

The candidate for delegate could make whatever pledges she or he considered appropriate. "I am inclined to be for Reagan, but could be for Baker, and could support Bush as we learn more about him. I might even go for Ford." Is not that how most of us think—certainly in the early stages of the sweepstakes? Or the delegate-candidate could pledge flatly for one candidate and promise to stay hitched regardless of later enlightenment. It would be up to the voters to choose their representative delegates, including those who might promise no more than, "I'll look over the field and vote the way that seems best to serve the nation." Would local issues be predominant? I believe the voters would be too serious for that to happen.

There are far more delegates than there are congressmen, so convention delegates could be elected from fairly small districts down to wards or legislative districts, although this is a determination that only the state parties can make. Democratic party rules presently require that delegates "shall be elected at the Congressional District level or lower."[13] Lower is better, and one delegate per district is even better and should be a requirement, for it would result in a delegation that would more accurately mirror the voter makeup and would provide a wholesome diversity without quotas or slating. If congressional districts were used, a district slate could be presented, informally or officially, providing assurance for a "balanced" group. On the other hand, it is likely that a delegate from a single district would be better known and possibly more trusted to be representative in voting.

Such thinking delegates could be chosen by an election or by a caucus; that would not make much difference. I prefer election because there is less chance of manipulation. The rules now permit a limited number of party leaders and elected officials to be selected at large; this provision need not be altered, although there are those people who believe that more party and public officials should be required to serve as delegates. One Democratic leader, John Hoving, has suggested that all public officials and party leaders should be required to be delegates as part of their official duties.[14]

Milton S. Eisenhower pointed out that "we have a representative form of government at every level—city, county, state, and federal. . . . In this light, my suggestion that delegates be selected as representatives of their constituencies, with considerable freedom to exercise their best judgment on the basis of evidence obtained at the convention, does not seem to me to be unreasonable or a departure from representational procedures."[15]

Supporters of particular presidential candidates could and surely would support partisans for the delegate positions. The discipline from a presidential candidate's headquarters also would tend to concentrate support on one candidate, so that six Smith delegate-candidates would not be killing off one another while running against a single Jones delegate-candidate. At the same time, the delegate-candidate who showed some independence might fare even better, especially in a situation in which the available presidential candidates cause many voters to want to mark their ballots for "none of the above."

This plea for thinking delegates is inherently fairer, more open and representative, than the present slating of a delegation favorable to one candidate. The voters' choices are presently too limited; they can look at two, sometimes several, slates—or candidates' names that will translate into slates—and take it or leave it, like it or lump it. The voter is entitled to a more influential vote, and the good of the republic demands it.

Selecting thinking delegates does not deny the presidential candidate the opportunity to gather in favorable delegates in advance of the convention. And surely no presidential candidate should be fearful of having the support of thinking delegates.

There could be some abuses in delegate selection. There are some abuses now. Campaign expenditures should be defined, and the party rules would need to limit, preferably prohibit, the spending of presidential campaign funds on behalf of individual delegate-candidates without full and timely disclosure. The best way to deal with this problem is, not by federal or state legislation, but by party rules. The party has the right to deny a seat to a delegate who has violated the rule dealing with campaign expenditures and to seat instead an alternate or the candidate who ran second to the offender; this is a far more persuasive deterrent than statutory sanctions.

There is another worry. Without a feeling of direct participation by actually voting for a presidential candidate or his designated slate, would there be any interest in such a campaign? Would the voters turn out? Would labor unions, teachers' associations, trade groups, the "electronic ministry," and other well-organized politically oriented organizations be able to override a light vote and distort the general will of the public? Would the voters disdain the uncommitted delegates? Would the uncommitted voters identify with the uncommitted delegates—uncommitted to what? Would the newspapers ridicule their arrogance in remaining uncommitted—"Who the hell do they think they are that they expect us to trust them?" Would candidates for delegate positions be well enough known to the voters?

These are not the only doubts that can be raised, but we cannot turn away from the task because of doubts. Restoration of a responsible nominating process demands change, so party leaders can think about all the doubts and guard against the flaws as they seek a system that would result in our getting thinking delegates. Perhaps delegates could be committed but not bound, with the general understanding that we know where they stand but want them to feel free to change their vote as best suits the nation. The various requirements that hold a delegate legally bound until released by a presidential candidate have little justification; the delegate is not a candidate's delegate—he or she should be the people's delegate.

Or, to pick up a lesson from 1912, could we allow individual states to bind their delegates to whatever degree the regional temperament demanded and then provide that winning on the first ballot (or the first two or three ballots) required a two-thirds (or maybe a 60-percent) vote? If no one were nominated after the first ballots, there would then be a convention of released and thinking delegates. Whatever the rules, it should not be too easy to win on the first ballot.

I argue not so much for a specific plan as for a plan by the parties that will achieve a deliberative convention of delegates free to think and act on behalf of the nation and their constituents. Of course there are doubts to be raised, but I believe that this objective of deliberation can be accomplished in a straightforward manner. Voters would elect delegates in whom they have confidence. Delegates would be responsible, responsive, and representative. I believe the voters are immensely disturbed by the present system and are ready to pay attention to a deliberative process of presidential nomination.

There is yet another important advantage to having thinking delegates. They could become *educated* delegates. That possibility would flow from the adoption of another principle that would enable us to know far more about the presidential candidates than we have known or are likely to know under the blitz-dash-flash-jump-run pattern of campaigning we presently endure.

SECOND PRINCIPLE: Achieve a contemplative convention by electing the delegates in time for them to meet with the candidates, in time for the candidates to electioneer with the delegates, and in time to allow the constituents ample opportunity to communicate with the delegates.

Although it is good to suppose that thinking delegates can be more deliberative in convention, the emotion, excitement, and immediacy of that occasion make careful examination and contemplation difficult. The delegates, most of them, will have established their preferences before leaving home, and although there can be additional learning and understanding through consorting with other delegates and through anticipated whirlwind delegation visits by the candidates, there is a better way to obtain a contemplative convention. The time frame for the election of delegates could be set so that all delegates would be chosen by a date some two months in advance of the national convention. Then the candidates, instead of dashing around to last-hour primaries, could be talking to the delegates who have been elected to examine them and, of greater importance, the delegates could, with greater objectivity, do what they were elected to do—find out all there is to know about all the candidates.

This change in the present rules could be easily accomplished. Taken hand in hand with the concept of representative delegates entrusted with democracy's decision, this proposed change would supply the missing essential ingredient to the process of nominating a presidential candidate.

We have not known very much about several of the recent presidential candidates until they had the nomination in hand. That they have turned out to be satisfactory is no excuse for allowing this dangerous flaw in the system to remain. An intense examination of candidates, their views and peculiarities, and their strengths and weaknesses is not today part of the presidential nomination scenario—to use an overworked word political organizers seem to like.

True we have occasional debates, but they do not tell us much. It is quite possible that the 1960 debates turned the tide against Richard Nixon, but although there were doubtless adequate reasons for the voters to reject Mr. Nixon, the fact that he sweated profusely and looked nervous when he was nervous was not one of them. True, we have televised question-and-answer shows that are helpful, but they cannot be exhaustive and seldom have been intense. There are articles in magazines and newspapers, but they are sporadic and ex parte.

The media do a fair job, but writers and publishers are not responsible for presenting a thorough analysis of each candidate's record, qualifications, and characteristics. The media should not be burdened with the job our convention delegates, duly and representatively elected, should be expected to shoulder.

As it is, the news media are gaining control of the process, something they cannot handle and do not want. They are at best reporters of things done and said, and their comrades who are columnists or TV anchormen with license to speculate and editorialize cannot do so deeply enough to provide much of educational value. What they do, even if helpful, is nonetheless fragmentary and sketchy. They also have been accused, with some justification, of having sheeplike or blackbird tendencies. Eugene McCarthy commented, "They reminded me of blackbirds on a telephone line. When one flies off, they all fly off. When one returns, they all return."[16]

During the extended time that all of this fragmented and scanty media educational process is going on, under the present rules more and more delegates are being elected and bound to vote in a way that makes their education about the candidates irrelevant to them and their constituents. With representative, thinking delegates elected two months in advance, we would institutionalize a system that would provide for deeper analysis, more thorough examination, and ample contemplation. The press could report more of factual performance and come to judgments and editorial opinions that would be better informed and in turn better inform the voting public.

The delegates would take on quite a task on their constituents' behalf. They would be bombarded by callers and campaign material; but road commissioners and school board members are also bombarded by constituents—it is a healthy part of democratic communication. The delegates would draw out information that in the past has not been called up. Each delegate could make a deliberate and thoughtful decision.

Certainly the rules would have to anticipate some abuses. It would be well to provide that candidates could spend no money on delegates, not even the cost of a meal and certainly not an airplane ticket. Let the state party buy the chicken and peas, or let the delegates pay individually if a meal is appropriate. Maybe the state parties should pay a per diem allowance to the delegates, which would be a healthy development anyhow; we need to ease the way for delegates with little money.

It would be well to provide that neither the candidates, nor friends, nor anyone else (except those people who have party funds for official travel) could transport the delegates to places of entertainment or even places of meeting. The relationship between delegates and candidates would need to be above reproach, which is not necessarily the case today for uncommitted delegates, since rules do not focus on this relationship. How to enforce? A violation would disqualify the delegate in favor of an alternate. Such shenanigans would also discredit a presidential candidate in the eyes of the other delegates. The press could, and would, publicize such indiscretions.

The state parties should schedule public meetings with each candidate for in-depth discussions and cross-examination. Quickie joint appearances of candidates would no longer be appropriate. In larger states the delegates could meet the candidates in smaller area groups. The state parties should also arrange public hearings to be conducted by the delegations to hear from the constituents about the candidates and to air the issues. There is also a platform to be adopted at the national convention. Such public hearings would mean that we would have a deliberative process that permitted the total party membership to participate.

Candidates could certainly send material to delegates, call them, and visit them, to whatever extent the candidates thought appropriate and the delegates thought acceptable. Constituents, too, could have a continuing dialogue with their delegates.

Sitting presidents who are challenged within their own party would be subject to close scrutiny and could not ignore the elected delegates. But incumbent presidents would not, unless they so chose, need to involve themselves in primary campaigns; they are already on display every day and have already proved their campaigning abilities. A president, as other candidates, could be called to account before duly elected representatives of the party but would not be subjected to the time-consuming task of personal campaigning state by state, a situation that is diverting and therefore dangerous.

All presidential candidates then would campaign precisely with the delegates with whom the decision rests but in full view of the public. The public and the constituents could directly influence the delegates as the public learned more about the several candidates. Such a procedure would permit a searching examination, something not now a part of the nominating process. Delegates would much more likely be "representative" when they arrived at the convention hall. That, too, is a radical change in concept.

THIRD PRINCIPLE: Provide for a participatory electorate that informs and guides the process but does not distort it.

To achieve this aim, we could keep all primaries any state wanted to keep but schedule them within time limits established by the parties and separate the primary election from the delegate selection process. This would be a radical change in most states.

Delegates would be elected on their representative merits, not slated on the basis of a primary vote. Campaigning in primaries, even if delegates were not gained there, would use the primary to its best advantage—displaying the talents and campaigning capacities of the person to be selected as the party's presidential candidate—and would avoid its principal disadvantage—locking in delegate votes on the basis of often inconclusive votes that reveal inexact directions as to voter interests.

151

The presidential primary performs an extremely important function. Making all presidential primaries *preferential* would be somewhat of a jolt for those people who think the primary is a reliable voice of democracy. Those who would contend that a "beauty contest" primary would attract little interest and fewer voters might be reminded that even the Florida straw votes of 1979, which had no legal effect and little logical meaning, had candidates and media people spending millions and swarming all over the state—and got many a federal project off the back burner. The nonbinding primary may attract even greater participation, because the voters will know why they are voting.

Those people who fear a candidate would not get what he "rightfully earned" might contemplate that the nation today stands in constant peril of getting what it does not deserve. It is apparent that we should not leave things as they are. Who among us cannot find serious inequities and dangers in the existing maze of primaries?

There are those people who favor regional primaries. I don't. I favor groupings of primaries. Regional primaries promote regionalism, of which we already have too much. I favor setting six primary days—designated Tuesdays in March and April. Either party could take this step and the other would follow. Then the individual state could pick a date if it wanted a primary. There is no necessity to have the primaries evenly divided among the designated dates, and it is preferable to have them scattered across the nation on each primary day.

These, then, are the three essential principles I recommend to provide a deliberative body of convention delegates who are in a position to know and reflect the views of their constituents and to examine carefully everything about every candidate. First, elect representative delegates who are free to think for themselves as guided by the generalized and communicated desires of those who elected them. Second, elect the delegates in time for them to become educated about the presidential candidates and give them an opportunity to listen to their constituents at length. Third, hold presidential primaries that guide and instruct but do not bind and distort.

The adoption of these principles would require radical, substantial changes and would call for determined party leadership to achieve them. They could provide new public assurances that the leader of our participatory society is being carefully chosen in the best republican tradition of our representative democracy.

Notes

1. Letter to author, April 28, 1980.
2. Jules Abels, *The Degeneration of Our Presidential Election: A History and Analysis of an American Institution in Trouble* (New York: Macmillan Company, 1968), p. 283.
3. Ibid., p. 306.
4. Judith H. Parris, *The Convention Problem: Issues in Reform of Presidential Nominating Procedures* (Washington, D.C.: Brookings Institution, 1972), pp. 12–15.
5. Ibid., p. 14.
6. Ibid., pp. 14–15.
7. Ibid., p. 177.
8. Ibid., p. 178.
9. Walter Lippmann, *The Essential Lippmann: A Political Philosophy for Liberal Democracy*, ed. Clinton Rossiter and James Lare (New York: Random House, 1963), p. 4.
10. Ibid., p. 26.
11. Walter Cronkite, "Changes I Have Seen in Political Conventions," in *1964 Guide to Conventions and Elections*, ed. Stanford M. Mirkin (New York: Dell Publishing Co. by Columbia Broadcasting System, 1964), p. 60.
12. See Jeane Kirkpatrick, *The New Presidential Elite: Men and Women in National Politics* (New York: Russell Sage Foundation, 1976), chapters 12, 13, 14.

13. *Delegate Selection Rules for the 1980 Democratic National Convention* by John C. White, Chairman (Washington, D.C.: Democratic National Committee, 1978), p. 9.

14. Letter to author, May 5, 1980.

15. Milton S. Eisenhower, *The President Is Calling* (Garden City, N.Y.: Doubleday & Company, 1974), pp. 401–403.

16. Eugene McCarthy, *The Year of the People* (Garden City, N.Y.: Doubleday & Company, 1969), p. 101.

15

Where To?

The United States has not solved enough of the problems of American society, and it has not come close enough to fulfilling its own promise and the aspirations we have for years collectively accepted as inevitable in this land of promise and opportunity.

We have settled for programs that give food and shelter, sporadically and meagerly, instead of opening up opportunity generously and as a matter of right. We have millions who are not oppressed and restrained, as are those people who live in societies that put less stock in human values, but who nonetheless find their lives wasted and futile and full of needless suffering and deprivation.

We have recently even found it difficult to manage the economic and societal environment for the affluent. The middle-income family finds it a strain to pay for college educations. The young and eager and hardworking find it too costly to buy a home. The economy runs its own rampant way without our being able to restrain, guide, or even understand it. Brutality threatens us, and institutional stupidity stifles us, and our national affairs are, or seem to be, totally out of hand.

We are no longer powerful enough to have our way in a dangerous world, and recent years have repeatedly demonstrated that our leadership is probably not wise enough to know what "our way" is anyhow.

Congress is unable to manage itself. The clumsiness of our bureaucracy endlessly and needlessly complicates our lives, and our insensitiveness to human failings and frailties makes us less than our tradition has promised. The inadequacies of our institutions appall us when we look up from our daily chores, and we cry out for vision and purpose and direction.

It is time that we shook ourselves by our own lapels and said, "Look here, this is a great nation, and we can do whatever we aspire to do." This revitalization must also take place beyond the public sector. Churches, labor unions, and so many other institutions are in need of self-renewal. Colleges and universities can become the innovative and challenging discoverers of values that they are supposed to be. Business can admit its secret concern for more than the "bottom line."

Political life is not the beginning and the end of our hope and accomplishments, but it is one activity that can involve every citizen, the one that affords a beginning point for national self-renewal. Political parties can be used to fulfill the people's responsibility to pick competent and imaginative leaders who can provide the government leadership we must have. Political parties are not the only way, I suppose, to mobilize the best of the political instincts of a nation, but until we design or even discuss a better instrument, we would do well to keep them functioning in place.

A president doesn't make or break our nation. We have had bad ones and have survived. But a president's leadership can be extremely important to our progress, to our individual well-being, to our national vision and inspiration, and to our slow steps forward. History often measures our societal progress by reference to a presidential administration. We cannot be satisfied to go about the duty of selecting a president in a haphazard manner.

There are fresh opportunities for all through the activities of political parties, but they are not going to be taken up and accomplished without our expression of will and purpose. Neither are they going to be achieved if blocked by selfishness. Further reforming of recent party reforms is not instantly embraced by groups who rightly feel that the accomplished reforms for the first time provide them access to a previously restricted club, and I can imagine some groups, say women, feeling threatened by further change. It is not a threat; it is a broadened opportunity for all of us.

There is much to be done in the United States. Our capacity is as strong as it was in 1787 when the Constitution was written, although shaping up our government may seem less compelling today. The times are more complex, leadership embraces almost everyone instead of a few elite people of the kind who gathered in Philadelphia, and the solutions are more difficult to define, but the stakes are the same. And our experience is far greater.

It is time for a reexamination of our political structures, their effectiveness and vitality, and specifically the responsibility for selecting presidential nominees. It is one starting point for the renewal of a mighty nation.

This book is not merely about rules for political parties and structures for making politics work. Or it is not intended to be. Carl Sandburg, some forty years ago, wrote "Good Morning, America," full of mirth and questions and faith and doubts.

> Now it's Uncle Sam sitting on top of the world.
> Not so long ago it was John Bull and, earlier yet,
>   Napoleon and the eagles of France told the world
>   where to get off at.
> Spain, Rome, Greece, Persia, their blunderbuss guns, their
>   spears, catapults, ships, took their turn at leading
>   the civilizations of the earth—

157

One by one they were bumped off, moved over, left behind,
    taken for a ride; they died or they lost the wallop
    they used to pack, not so good, not so good.
One by one they no longer sat on top of the world—now
    the Young Stranger is Uncle Sam, is America and the
    song goes, "The stars and stripes forever!" even
    though "forever" is a long time.[1]

Also some forty years ago, young Thomas Wolfe of North Carolina, in a New York flat, tormented and sweating and striving, having lived through America's Great Depression until the landfall was in sight, wrote:

> I believe that we are lost here in America, but I believe we shall be found. And this belief, which mounts now to the catharsis of knowledge and conviction, is for me—and I think for all of us—not only our own hope, but America's everlasting, living dream. . . . I think the true discovery of America is before us. I think the true fulfillment of our spirit, of our people, of our mighty and immortal land, is yet to come. I think the true discovery of our own democracy is still before us.[2]

And so it is.

Notes

1. Carl Sandburg, "Good Morning, America," in *Complete Poems of Carl Sandburg* (New York: Harcourt Brace Jovanovich, Inc., 1950), p. 332, stanza 14.
2. Thomas Wolfe, *You Can't Go Home Again* (Garden City, N.Y.: Sun Dial Press, 1942), p. 741.

APPENDIX
Approval Voting: A Practical Reform for Multicandidate Elections
Stephen J. Brams

Approval voting is a system in which a voter may choose or approve of as many candidates as desired in a multicandidate election. For example, a voter might vote for just one candidate, or for several candidates if more than one is found acceptable. However, only one vote may be cast for every approved candidate—that is, votes may not be cumulated and several cast for one candidate. The candidate with the most votes wins.

With approval voting, two or more candidates each could receive the votes of more than 50 percent of the voters, though in a large field of candidates such an outcome would probably be unlikely. Even so, the thought that more than one candidate could be supported by a majority of voters does seem strange. So does the idea of giving voters the opportunity to vote for more than one candidate that can produce this result. Yet, approval voting is not only compatible with most constitutions but it also has several advan-

From *National Civic Review* 68:10 (New York: National Municipal League, November 1979). Reprinted by permission.

tages over plurality voting, plurality voting with a runoff (if no candidate receives a majority in the first election), and preferential voting (in which voters can rank candidates). Moreover, it is practical: among other things, it can readily be implemented on existing voting machines, and it is more efficient than holding both a plurality and runoff election.

Here are the main arguments for approval voting:

1. *It is best for the voters.* Approval voting allows citizens to do exactly what they do now—vote for their favorite candidate—but, if they have no clear favorite, it also allows them to express this fact by voting for all candidates that they rank highest. In addition, if a favorite seems to have little chance of winning, the voter can still cast a ballot for that candidate without worrying about "wasting one's vote." This is done by voting for the favorite *and* the candidate considered most acceptable who seems to have a serious chance of winning. This way a voter is able to express a sincere preference and at the same time vote for the candidate who would be preferable if the favorite cannot win.

Apart from the question of wasting one's vote, plurality voting is fundamentally unfair to a voter who may have a hard time deciding who is the best candidate in a crowded field but can choose the two or more candidates considered most acceptable. Approval voting thus provides more flexible options and thereby encourages a truer expression of preferences than does plurality voting.

2. *It elects the strongest candidate.* It is entirely possible in a three-candidate plurality race in which A wins 25 percent of the vote, B 35 percent and C 40 percent that the loser, A, is the strongest candidate who would beat B in a separate two-way contest (because C supporters would vote for A), and would beat C in a separate two-way contest (because B supporters would vote for A). Even a runoff election between the top vote getters (B and C) would not show up this fact. On the other hand, approval voting in all likelihood would reveal A to be the strongest candidate because some B and C

supporters—who liked A as much or almost as much—would cast second approval votes for A, who would thereby become the winner.

It is not hard to think of actual elections in which minority candidates triumphed with less than 50 percent of the vote who almost surely would have lost if they had been in contests with just one of their opponents. For example, a liberal, John Lindsay, won the 1969 mayoral election in New York City against two opponents who split the moderate-conservative vote (58 percent of the total); and a conservative James Buckley won the 1970 U.S. Senate election in New York against two opponents who split the moderate-liberal vote (61 percent of the total). This problem of a minority candidate's eking out a victory in a crowded field is aggravated the more candidates there are in a race. Moreover, as the examples indicate, the minority-candidate bias of plurality voting is not ideological: it can afflict both liberals and conservatives. Approval voting, by contrast, is biased in favor of the strongest candidate, especially a candidate like A in the earlier example who would defeat each of the others in head-to-head contests.

3. *It is best for the parties.* For reasons just given, approval voting would tend to favor the strongest and most viable candidates in each party. It is unlikely, for example, that Barry Goldwater would have won the Republican presidential nomination in 1964, or George McGovern the Democratic presidential nomination in 1972, if there had been approval voting in the state presidential primaries. Both nominees were probably minority candidates even within their own parties, and both lost decisively in the general election.

4. *It gives minority candidates their proper due.* In 1968, George Wallace dropped from 21 percent support in the polls in September to 14 percent in the actual vote on election day in November. It seems likely that the one-third of Wallace supporters who deserted him in favor of one of the major-party candidates did so because they thought he had no serious chance of winning—the wasted vote phenomenon.

But, if there had been approval voting, Wallace would almost surely have retained his original supporters, some of whom would also have voted for Nixon or Humphrey. One of these candidates would have won, probably with more than 50 percent of the vote (Nixon received 43.4 percent in the election; Humphrey, 42.7 percent), but Wallace would have registered much more substantial support than he did. With approval voting, minority candidates would get their proper due, but majority candidates would generally win.

5. *It is insensitive to the number of candidates running*. Because ballots may be cast for as many candidates as the voter wishes under approval voting, if new candidates enter it is still possible to vote for one or more of them without being forced to withdraw support from old candidates. Plurality voting, on the other hand, is very sensitive to the number of candidates running. As the number of contenders increases, the plurality contest becomes more and more one of who can inch out whom in a crowded field rather than who is the strongest and most acceptable candidate.

Thus, when Jimmy Carter won less than 30 percent of the vote in the New Hampshire Democratic primary in 1976, the significance of his victory could be questioned. This gave the media an opportunity to pass judgment, which they gleefully did. Approval voting, by contrast, by better revealing the overall acceptability of the candidates independent of the field in which they run, more accurately mirrors each candidate's true level of support and gives more meaning to the voter's judgment. A side benefit would be that the voters, not the media, would weigh in more heavily in the selection process.

As an example of a recent election in which the overall acceptability of candidates was difficult to ascertain, consider the Democratic primary in the 1977 New York City mayoral election. With no candidate receiving as much as 20 percent of the vote, and six candidates receiving more than 10 percent, a judgment about who the most popular candidate was seems highly dubious. Even the runoff election that pitted Edward Koch (19.8 percent of the plurality vote) against Mario Cuomo (18.6 percent of the plurality vote) said nothing about how the winner, Koch, would have fared in runoffs against the other four candidates who received between 11.0 and 18.0 percent of the plurality vote. Although Koch may have been the candidate more acceptable to the voters than any other candidate in this election, plurality voting, even with a runoff, did not demonstrate this to be the case.

An Example. The following hypothetical example perhaps best dramatizes the different effects of plurality voting and approval voting:

	Plurality Voting	Approval Voting
Candidate X	25%	30%
Candidate Y	24%	51%

In this example, which assumes X and Y are the top two candidates in the race and several other candidates split the remaining vote, X just wins under plurality voting. Yet X is approved of by less than one-third of the voters, whereas Y is acceptable to more than one-half of the voters.

Is it fair that X, unacceptable to 70 percent of the electorate, should be considered the "winner" simply because he is the first choice of more voters than any other candidate in a crowded field? He may be liked by the biggest minority of voters (25 percent), but in my opinion the voting system should also register the fact that he is disliked—that is, not approved of—by all but 30 percent of the voters.

Approval voting would show up the fact that Y is acceptable to many more voters than X. Of course, the plurality voting winner and the approval voting winner will often be the same, and then there will be no problem. However, the discrepancy between plurality and approval voting winners seems not so infrequent, even in races with as few as three candidates, to be dismissed as a rare event.

APPENDIX

6. *It could increase voter turnout.* By giving voters more flexible options, approval voting could encourage greater voter turnout, although this is difficult to establish until we have some experience with approval voting. It seems likely, however, that some voters do not go to the polls because they cannot make up their minds about who is the single best candidate in a multi-candidate race. By giving such voters the option to vote for two or more candidates if they have no clear favorite, they probably would have more incentive to vote in the first place.

7. *It is superior to preferential voting.* An election reform that has been tried in a few places in the United States (for example, Ann Arbor, Michigan) shares many of the advantages of approval voting. It is called preferential voting and it requires each voter to rank the candidates from best to worst. If no candidate receives a majority of first-place votes, the candidate with the fewest first-place votes is dropped and the second-place votes of his supporters are given to the remaining candidates. The elimination process continues, with lower-place votes of the voters whose preferred candidates are eliminated being transferred to the candidates that survive, until one candidate receives a majority of votes.

Apart from the practical problems of implementing a ranking system, preferential voting has a major drawback: it may eliminate the candidate acceptable to the most voters. In the hypothetical example given in argument 2 above, A would have been eliminated at the outset. Yet, A would have defeated B and C in separate two-way contests, and was, therefore, the strongest candidate and probably would have won with approval voting.

A less serious drawback of preferential voting is that the candidate with the most first-place votes may be displaced after the transfers have been made to determine the majority winner. This may greatly upset that candidate's supporters, particularly if they are a large minority, and lead to questions about the legitimacy of the system. This challenge cannot be mounted against approval voting since approval votes are in-distinguishable—whether these votes are first-place, second-place, or whatever is not recorded, so no portion of the winner's total can be judged "inferior."

8. *Practicalities*. It may be thought that, even given the virtues of approval voting, it would make little difference in a real election. This is so because the candidates would encourage voters to vote just for themselves (bullet voting) to keep down the vote totals of their opponents. Yet, even if the candidates made such an appeal, it would probably not be effective, particularly in a crowded race in which voters had difficulty distinguishing their single favorite. As evidence to support this assertion, in an approval voting experiment involving several hundred Pennsylvania voters prior to their 1976 primaries, 72 percent of the voters voted for two or more of the eight candidates listed on their sample ballots.

How can approval voting be implemented? There are a multitude of laws governing the conduct of elections, but consider the statute in New Hampshire for voting in the presidential primaries. To enact approval voting in these elections would require only the substitution of the words in parentheses for the preceding words:

> Every qualified voter . . . shall have opportunity . . . to vote his preference (preferences), on the ballot of his party, for his choice (choices) for one person (any persons) to be the candidate (candidates) of his political party for president of the United States and one person (any persons) to be the candidate (candidates) of his political party for vice president of the United States.

I have been assured by voting machine manufacturers that their equipment could be easily adjusted to allow for approval voting. In jurisdictions which use paper ballots, allowing voters to mark their ballots for more than one candidate will make vote counting somewhat more tedious and time-consuming, but this should not be a major barrier to the adoption of approval voting.

I am completely convinced that approval voting will be the election reform of the 20th century, just as the Australian, or secret, ballot printed by the government with the names of all authorized candidates was the election reform of the 19th century. In effect, the principle of "one man, one vote" in plurality voting becomes the principle of "one candidate, one vote" with approval voting.

Selected Bibliography

Abels, Jules. *The Degeneration of Our Presidential Election: A History and Analysis of an American Institution in Trouble.* New York: Macmillan Company, 1968.

Anderson, Jack, and Blumenthal, Fred. *The Kefauver Story.* New York: Dial Press, 1956.

Arterton, F. Christopher. "Strategies and Tactics of Candidate Organizations," *Political Science Quarterly* 92 (Winter 1977–1978):663–671.

Baar, Carl, and Baar, Ellen. "Party and Convention Organization and Leadership Selection in Canada and the United States." In *Perspectives on Presidential Selection*, edited by Donald R. Matthews, pp. 49–84. Washington, D.C.: Brookings Institution, 1973.

Bain, Richard C., and Parris, Judith H. *Convention Decisions and Voting Records.* 2d ed. Washington, D.C.: Brookings Institution, 1973.

Barber, James David. *The Presidential Character: Predicting Performance in the White House.* 2d ed. Englewood Cliffs, N.J.: Prentice-Hall, 1977.

____. *The Pulse of Politics: Electing Presidents in the Media Age.* New York: W. W. Norton & Company, 1980.

____. "This Year, Why Not the Facts?" *New York Times*, 17 March 1980, sec. A, p. 19.

Barber, James David, ed. *Choosing the President*. Englewood Cliffs, N.J.: Prentice-Hall, 1974.

Baron, Alan. "Inside: Analysis of the Democratic and Republican Presidential Races—and the November Election." *Baron Report*, 23 January 1980.

____. "Special Report on 1980 House Races and A Guide to How the Iowa Caucus System Works." *Baron Report*, 9 January 1980.

Best, Judith. *The Case Against Direct Election of the President: A Defense of the Electoral College*. Ithaca: Cornell University Press, 1971.

Bickel, Alexander M. *Reform and Continuity: The Electoral College, the Convention, and the Party System*. New York: Harper & Row, 1968.

Bishop, Joseph Bucklin. *Presidential Nominations and Elections*. New York: Charles Scribner's Sons, 1916.

Brams, Steven J. *The Presidential Election Game*. New Haven: Yale University Press, 1978.

Brerton, Charles. *First Step to the White House: The New Hampshire Primary 1952-1980*. Hampton, N.H.: Wheelabrator Foundation, 1979.

Broder, David S. "A Better Choice of Presidents." *Washington Post*, 29 August 1979, sec. A, p. 25.

____. *The Party's Over: The Failure of Politics in America*. New York: Harper & Row, 1971.

____. "Primaries Full of Paradox." *The News and Observer*, Raleigh, North Carolina, 9 June 1976, p. 5.

Burns, James MacGregor. *The Deadlock of Democracy*. Englewood Cliffs, N.J.: Prentice-Hall, 1963.

Casey, Carol F. *Procedures for Selection of Delegates to the Democratic and Republican 1980 Conventions: A Survey of Applicable State Laws and Party Rules*. Washington, D.C.: Library of Congress, Congressional Research Service, 22 October 1979.

Casey, John T., and Bowles, James. *Farley and Tomorrow*. Chicago: Reilly & Lee Co., 1937.

"Casual Joe Takes a Fall." *Time*, 24 December 1979, p. 32.

Charles, Joseph. *The Origins of the American Party System*. New York: Harper & Row, 1956.

Chase, James S. *Emergence of the Presidential Nominating Convention 1789-1832*. Urbana: University of Illinois Press, 1973.

Cook, Rhodes. "Presidential Primaries Reach Record Level." *Congressional Quarterly*, 4 August 1979, pp. 1609-1616.

Cronkite, Walter. "Changes I Have Seen in Political Conventions." In *1964 Guide to Conventions and Elections*, edited by Stanford M. Mirkin, pp. 60-63. New York: Dell Publishing Company by Columbia Broadcasting System, 1964.

Crotty, William J. *Political Reform and the American Experiment*. New York: Thomas Y. Crowell Company, 1977.

Cunningham, Noble E., Jr. "Election of 1800." In *History of American Presidential Elections*, vol. 1, *1789-1844*, edited by Arthur M. Schlesinger, Jr., pp. 105-155. New York: Chelsea House Publishers, 1971.

David, Paul T.; Goldman, Ralph M.; and Bain, Richard C. *The Politics of National Party Conventions*. Washington, D.C.: Brookings Institution, 1960.

Davis, James W. *Presidential Primaries: Road to the White House*. New York: Thomas Y. Crowell Company, 1967.

Delegate Selection Rules for the 1980 Democratic National Convention by John C. White, Chairman. Washington, D.C.: Democratic National Committee, 1978.

Eaton, Herbert. *Presidential Timber: A History of Nominating Conventions, 1869-1960*. New York: Free Press of Glencoe, 1964.

Eisenhower, Dwight D. "Our National Nominating Conventions Are a Disgrace." *Reader's Digest*, July 1966, pp. 76-80.

Eisenhower, Milton S. *The President Is Calling*. Garden City, N.Y.: Doubleday & Company, 1974.

SELECTED BIBLIOGRAPHY

Epstein, Leon D. "Political Science and Presidential Nominations."
Political Science Quarterly 93 (Summer 1978):177–195.

Farley, James A. *Behind the Ballots*. New York: Harcourt, Brace and
Company, 1938.

Garson, Robert A. *The Democratic Party and the Politics of Sectional-
ism, 1941-1948*. Baton Rouge: Louisiana State University Press, 1974.

Germond, Jack W., and Witcover, Jules. "Hectic Primary Pace Precludes
Cognitive Weeding Out." *The News and Observer,* Raleigh, North
Carolina, 28 March 1980, p. 5.

Gillette, William. "Election of 1872." In *History of American Presidential Elections*, vol. 2, *1848-1896*, edited by Arthur M. Schlesinger,
Jr., pp. 1303–1374. New York: Chelsea House Publishers, 1971.

Goodman, William. *The Two-Party System in the United States*. Princeton, N.J.: D. Van Nostrand Company, 1956.

Goodwyn, Lawrence. *Democratic Promise: The Populist Moment in
America*. New York: Oxford University Press, 1976.

Gorman, Joseph Bruce. *Kefauver: A Political Biography*. New York:
Oxford University Press, 1971.

Graham, Frank. *Al Smith: American*. New York: G. P. Putnam's Sons,
1945.

Handlin, Oscar. *Al Smith and His America*. Boston: Little, Brown and
Company, 1958.

Hess, Stephen. *The Presidential Campaign: The Leadership Selection
Process After Watergate*. Washington, D.C.: Brookings Institution,
1974.

Hopkins, James F. "Election of 1824." In *History of Presidential
Elections*, vol. 1, *1789-1844*, edited by Arthur M. Schlesinger, Jr.,
pp. 349–408. New York: Chelsea House Publishers, 1971.

Hutchins, Robert Maynard, ed. *Great Books of the Western World*. Vol.
43, *American State Papers, The Federalist, J. S. Mill*. Chicago:
Encyclopaedia Britannica, 1952.

"Is There a Better Method of Picking Presidential Nominees?" *New*

170

York Times, 2 December 1979, sec. 4, p. E5.

Keech, William R., and Matthews, Donald R. *The Party's Choice.* Washington, D.C.: Brookings Institution, 1976.

Kennedy, John F. Inaugural Address. In Theodore C. Sorensen, *Kennedy,* pp. 245–248. New York: Harper & Row, 1965.

Kent, Frank R. *The Democratic Party: A History.* New York: Century Company, 1928.

Key, V. O., Jr. *Politics, Parties & Pressure Groups.* 5th ed. New York: Thomas Y. Crowell Company, 1964.

____. *The Responsible Electorate.* Cambridge: Belknap Press of Harvard University Press, 1966.

Kimmett, J. S., comp. *Nomination and Election of the President and Vice President of the United States.* Washington, D.C.: Government Printing Office, 1980.

King, Anthony. "The American Polity in the Late 1970s: Building Coalitions in the Sand." In *The New American Political System,* edited by Anthony King, pp. 371–395. Washington, D.C.: American Enterprise Institute for Public Policy Research, 1979.

King, Anthony, ed. *The New American Political System.* Washington, D.C.: American Enterprise Institute for Public Policy Research, 1979.

Kirkpatrick, Jeane. *The New Presidential Elite: Men and Women in National Politics.* New York: Russell Sage Foundation, 1976.

Kraus, Sidney, ed. *The Great Debates.* Bloomington: Indiana University Press, 1962.

Ladd, Everett Carll, Jr. " 'Reform' Is Wrecking the U.S. Party System." *Fortune,* November 1977, pp. 177–188.

Ladd, Everett Carll, Jr., and Hadley, Charles D. *Transformations of the American Party System: Political Coalitions from the New Deal to the 1970s.* 2d ed. New York: W. W. Norton & Company, 1978.

Lawson, Kay. *Political Parties and Democracy in the United States.* New York: Charles Scribner's Sons, 1968.

Lippmann, Walter. *The Essential Lippmann: A Political Philosophy for Liberal Democracy.* Edited by Clinton Rossiter and James Lare. New York: Random House, 1963.

Lubell, Samuel. *The Future of American Politics.* New York: Harper & Brothers, 1951.

McAdoo, William G. *Crowded Years.* Boston: Houghton Mifflin Company, 1931.

McCarthy, Charles. "The Antimasonic Party: A Study of Political Anti-Masonry in the United States, 1827–1840." Vol. 1, *Annual Report of the American Historical Association for the Year 1902*, pp. 365–574. Washington, D.C.: Government Printing Office, 1903.

McCarthy, Eugene. *The Year of the People.* Garden City, N.Y.: Doubleday & Company, 1969.

McClosky, Herbert; Hoffman, Paul J.; and O'Hara, Rosemary. "Issue Conflict and Consensus Among Party Leaders and Followers." *American Political Science Review* 54 (1960):406–427.

McGinniss, Joe. *The Selling of the President 1968.* New York: Trident Press, 1969.

McGovern, George. *Grassroots.* New York: Random House, 1977.

Matthews, Donald R., ed. *Perspectives on Presidential Selection.* Washington, D.C.: Brookings Institution, 1973.

Maxa, Rudy. "Front Page People." *Washington Post Magazine*, 20 January 1980, p. 4.

Merriam, Charles Edward, and Overracker, Louise. *Primary Elections.* Chicago: University of Chicago Press, 1928.

Minow, Newton N. "A Poor Primary System." *Wall Street Journal*, 13 August 1979, p. 14.

Mirkin, Stanford M., ed. *1964 Guide to Conventions and Elections.* New York: Dell Publishing Co. by Columbia Broadcasting System, 1964.

Nevins, Allan. *The Diary of John Quincy Adams, 1794–1845.* New York: Longmans, Green and Company, 1928.

"None of the Above." *New York Times*, 13 March 1980, sec. A, p. 22.

Ogden, Daniel M., Jr., and Peterson, Arthur L. *Electing the President*. Rev. ed. San Francisco: Chandler Publishing Company, 1968.

Openness, Participation and Party Building: Reforms for a Stronger Democratic Party by Morley A. Winograd, Chairman, Commission on Presidential Nomination and Party Structure. Washington, D.C.: Democratic National Committee, 1978.

Parris, Judith H. *The Convention Problem: Issues in Reform of Presidential Nominating Procedures*. Washington, D.C.: Brookings Institution, 1972.

Perkins, Frances. *The Roosevelt I Knew*. New York: Viking Press, 1946.

"Political Machinery and Windmills." *New York Times,* 20 March 1980, p. A26.

Polsby, Nelson W., and Wildavsky, Aaron B. *Presidential Elections: Strategies of American Electoral Politics*. New York: Charles Scribner's Sons, 1964.

____. *Strategies of American Electoral Politics: Presidential Elections*. 3d ed. New York: Charles Scribner's Sons, 1971.

Pomper, Gerald. *Nominating the President*. Evanston, Ill.: Northwestern University Press, 1963.

"President and Reagan Now Appear Likely Contenders in Fall Elections." *New York Times*, 20 March 1980, p. A1.

Ranney, Austin. *Curing the Mischiefs of Faction: Party Reform in America*. Los Angeles: University of California Press, 1975.

____. "The Political Parties: Reform and Decline." In *The New American Political System*, edited by Anthony King, pp. 213–247. Washington, D.C.: American Enterprise Institute for Public Policy Research, 1979.

Ranney, Austin, and Kendall, Willmoore. *Democracy and the American Party System*. Westport, Conn.: Greenwood Press, 1956.

Remini, Robert V. *Andrew Jackson*. New York: Twayne Publishers, 1966.

____. "Election of 1832." In *History of American Presidential Elections*, vol. 1, *1789-1844*, edited by Arthur M. Schlesinger, Jr., pp. 495-574. New York: Chelsea House Publishers, 1971.

Ribicoff, Abraham, and Newman, Jon O. *Politics: The American Way.* Boston: Allyn & Bacon, 1967.

Roseboom, Eugene H. *A History of Presidential Elections.* 3d ed. London: Macmillan Company, 1970.

Rossiter, Clinton, and Lare, James, eds. *The Essential Lippmann: A Political Philosophy for Liberal Democracy.* New York: Random House, 1963.

Rules Adopted by the 1976 Republican National Convention. Kansas City, Mo.: Lowell Press, 1976.

Saloma, John S., III, and Sontag, Frederick H. *Parties: The Real Opportunity for Effective Citizen Politics.* New York: Alfred A. Knopf, 1972.

Sayre, Wallace S., and Parris, Judith H. *Voting for President: The Electoral College and the American Political System.* Washington, D.C.: Brookings Institution, 1970.

Scheer, Julian. "New Hampshire Looks Candidates in the Eye." *The News and Observer,* Raleigh, North Carolina, 27 February 1980, p. 4.

Schlesinger, Arthur M., Jr. *The Age of Jackson.* Boston: Little, Brown and Company, 1946.

____. *The Age of Roosevelt.* Boston: Houghton Mifflin Company, 1960.

____. *The Coming of the New Deal.* Boston: Houghton Mifflin Company, 1959.

____. *The Crisis of the Old Order: 1919-1933.* Boston: Houghton Mifflin Company, 1957.

____. "Crisis of the Party System: I." *Wall Street Journal,* 10 May 1979, p. 30.

____. "Crisis of the Party System: II." *Wall Street Journal,* 14 May 1979, p. 20.

Schlesinger, Arthur M., Jr., ed. *History of American Presidential Elec-*

tions. Vol. 1, *1789–1844.* New York: Chelsea House Publishers, 1971.

____. *History of American Presidential Elections.* Vol. 2, *1848–1896.* New York: Chelsea House Publishers, 1971.

Smith, Page. "Election of 1796." In *History of American Presidential Elections,* vol. 1, *1789–1844,* edited by Arthur M. Schlesinger, Jr., pp. 59–98. New York: Chelsea House Publishers, 1971.

____. *John Adams.* Vol. 2, *1784–1826.* Garden City, N.Y.: Doubleday & Company, 1963.

Smith, T. V. *The Promise of American Politics.* 2d ed. Chicago: University of Chicago Press, 1936.

Sorauf, Frank J. *Party Politics in America.* Boston: Little, Brown and Company, 1968.

Sorensen, Theodore C. *Kennedy.* New York: Harper & Row, 1965.

Stanwood, Edward. *A History of the Presidency from 1788 to 1897.* New York: Houghton Mifflin Company, 1898.

____. *A History of the Presidency from 1897 to 1916.* Boston and New York: Houghton Mifflin Company, 1912.

Tillett, Paul, ed. *Inside Politics: The National Conventions, 1960.* Dobbs Ferry, N.Y.: Oceana Publications, 1962.

"Toward Reform of the Reforms." *Time,* 28 January 1980, pp. 26–27.

Truman, Harry S. *Memoirs.* Vol. 2, *Years of Trial and Hope.* Garden City, N.Y.: Doubleday & Company, 1956.

Tugwell, Rexford G. *Off Course: From Truman to Nixon.* New York: Praeger Publishers, 1971.

U.S. *Constitution.* Art. II, sec. 1.

U.S., Congress, House. *Report of Commission on the Democratic Selection of Presidential Nominees.* 90th Cong., 2d sess., 14 October 1968. *Congressional Record,* vol. 114.

Valeo, Francis R., comp. *Nomination and Election of the President and Vice President of the United States.* Washington, D.C.: Government Printing Office, 1976.

White, Theodore H. "The Making of the President Ain't What It Used to Be." *Life*, February 1980, pp. 66–80.

____. *The Making of the President 1964*. New York: Atheneum Publishers, 1965.

____. *The Making of the President 1968*. New York: Atheneum Publishers, 1969.

____. *The Making of the President 1972*. New York: Atheneum Publishers, 1973.

White, William Allen. *Politics: The Citizen's Business*. New York: Macmillan Company, 1924.

Witcover, Jules. "Rancor Grips Close GOP Race After Debate." *Washington Star*, 25 February 1980, p. A3.

Worldmark Encyclopedia of the Nations. "United Kingdom." 3d ed. New York: Worldmark Press, Harper & Row, 1967.

Index